THE LEGEND OF SAWNEY BEAN

Frontispiece: With the kind permission of the Trustees of the National Library of Scotland.

Sawney Beane *at the Entrance of his* CAVE.

RONALD HOLMES

THE LEGEND OF SAWNEY BEAN

"Ancient traditions, when tested by the severe process of modern investigation, commonly enough fade away into mere dreams, but it is singular how often the dream turns out to have been a half-awake one, presaging reality."

T H Huxley

FREDERICK MULLER LIMITED

First published in Great Britain 1975 by
Frederick Muller Ltd., London NW2 6LE

ISBN 0 584 10156 2

Set in Intertype Plantin
Printed in Great Britain by The Anchor Press Ltd
and bound by Wm Brendon & Son Ltd
both of Tiptree, Essex

Contents

By the same author

WITCHCRAFT IN BRITISH HISTORY

Introduction

The legend of Sawney Bean has exerted a strange fascination over those who have heard or read it since it was first published about the year 1700. It has never been out of print and, since that time, the theme has frequently been adapted by other writers until as recently as 1969 when the play *Sawney Bean* was produced. Undoubtedly its main fascination is the central theme of cannibalism which sends a chill through the very bones of the reader and puts it on a par with similar stories of vampires, werewolves and other monsters. But this is only part of the reason for its popularity.

The legend portrays Sawney Bean as a criminal and mass-murderer who was executed about the year 1600. There are, however, no records or other supporting evidence to prove that he really existed. This book is a work of detection which sets out to solve a murder mystery but, in so doing, displays Sawney Bean not so much as a criminal but as a primeval presence from the dark past of the human mind.

Evidence has been taken from the writings of many persons since the beginning of written history in Britain; and before that time evidence has been obtained from archaeologists and folklore. Over a hundred years ago Sabine Baring-Gould indicated the importance of the folk-tale in helping to complete the gaps in our knowledge of the history of man before the art of writing was developed.

> It is only of late years that household tales have been regarded

> as of interest by men of learning. For long they were thought to be "milk for babes", but to have nothing in them which could repay a moment's study by one who had emerged from childhood. But the great Grimm saw that in these stories for children lay fragments of ancient mythology, and he learned to trace them from land to land, and thus proved them to be precious heirlooms, derived from our primeval ancestors before they parted into separate nationalities. The mine was discovered by Grimm, others have gathered ore from it, but none have thoroughly worked it out, tracing its veins, and exhausting its stores of mythological wealth.

The recent discoveries of archaeologists have added to and confirmed much of the work of folk-lorists and it is only now, with the aid of this new information, that an analysis of the legend of Sawney Bean can be attempted with any hope of success.

Because the legend of Sawney Bean has grown from the culture and history of Galloway, there is much in this book about the south-west of Scotland and the term Galloway has been used to imply the whole of the area, as it formerly did, rather than the present County. There are included many folk-tales of this area which, unlike Sawney Bean, have not seen print for at least a hundred years and which deserve to be perpetuated for other reasons. These stories, together with others from all over Britain, when co-related with archaeological evidence, provide information which throws new light on the legend of Sawney Bean.

The term *Celtic* is used throughout this book in its widest sense. The term was first coined in the fifteenth century and was intended to embrace all those who spoke the Gaelic tongue, but since that time other connotations have been added. These are of little importance here, but the following quotation from Sir J. Rhys may clarify the matter.

> It is a long time ago since the first Celts crossed the sea to settle in Britain. Nobody knows how long, so the guesses which have been made as to the date are hardly worth recording. And when they did come the immigration was not all over in one year or even one century. The invasion may, however, be grouped into two, and may be looked at as made by peoples of both branches of the Celtic family. . . . To the one belonged the

> ancestors of the people who speak Gaelic in Ireland, the Isles of Man, and the Highlands of the North, a language which existed also in Wales and Devon in the sixth century, and probably later....
>
> But Galloway and Northumbria remained connected, after a fashion, long afterwards—probably until the former was bestowed with Cumbria on the king of the Scots by the English king Eadmund. Not only did these picts so far retain the individuality of their race as to be known by that name as late as the twelfth century . . . but there is no lack of evidence that they still clung, some four centuries later, to their Goidelic speech, which Scotch authors used to call Erch or Irische, as they rightly identified it with the Celtic language of Ireland and the Highlands.

In archaeological terms, these were the Iron-Age 'A' and Iron-Age 'B' peoples who over-ran Britain and absorbed the original inhabitants. Such fine distinctions are superfluous in this book and it should be understood that the terms *Celtic* and *Celt* are applied to the mixture of peoples which lived in the areas stated between the first Iron-Age invasion and the coming of the feudal system. We are concerned here with the *continuity* of beliefs which were handed from generation to generation during these centuries. The people may have changed the ethnological structure of their tribes by inter-marriage, enslavement and migration but before the coming of Christianity, so far as we can detect at this late date, their beliefs evolved very slowly indeed.

Because of the basic theme of this book it has been necessary to exclude many aspects of the culture of Galloway which are of a romantic or gentle nature. The author, who has come to admire the country and respect its people, regrets the inevitability of this and in the hope of reminding the reader that there is much more to be known and understood the following gem is reprinted from MacTaggart.

> Jock Mulldroch—A fellow who lived at Craigwaggie, Galloway. Tradition says that he laid eggs, ay eggs, larger than goose eggs, and strangely spreckled black and yellow; he used to cackle too after he laid them. Once a fortnight he is said to have produced an egg, and his mother, after having sold a few of them as bonny goose eggs, set a couple of them beneath a braw hen to hatch. Long and dreich did the favourite hen of Lucky Mulldroch sit on them before they were hatched; at length they chipped, and

out came two little lads clad in green, and under the goodwife's care they thrave, and were well known long over the south of Scotland by the title of the Birlies. Willie and Wattie Birly were well liked by everybody; they were something in the nature of brownies, or rather mongrell fairies. They vanished away though, after the year forty, the year of the long storm, they never were heard of; some think they sank in a snow drift, and afterwards into a quagmire.

Ryton-upon-Tyne
1974.

I

The Legend of Sawney Bean

No grief-speaking tear o'er his cheeks ever strayed,
From his hovel, that knew not the sun's cheering light,
He darted at once on the poor passing wight,
And stretched him in death by the Dee's rolling tide.

R. MALCOLMSON, *Black Murray*

(from a collection of legends entitled *Historical and Traditional Tales connected with the South of Scotland*—1843)

The following account, though as well attested as any historical fact can be, is almost incredible, for the monstrous and unparalleled barbarities that it relates; there being nothing that we ever heard of, with the same degree of certainty, that may be compared with it, or that shews how far a brutal temper, untamed by education, and knowledge of the world, may carry a man in such glaring and horrible colours.

Sawney Bean was born in the county of East Lothian, about eight miles eastward of the city of Edinburgh, in the reign of James I of Scotland. His father was a hedger and ditcher and brought up his son to the same laborious employment.

He got his daily bread in his youth by these means, but being very prone to idleness, and not caring to be confined to any honest employment, he left his father and mother, and ran away into the desert part of the country, taking with him a woman as viciously inclined as himself.

These two took up their habitation in a cave, by the sea-side on the shore of the county of Galloway; where they lived upwards of twenty-five years without ever going into any city, town or village.

In this time they had a great number of children and grand-children, whom they brought up after their own manner, without any notions of humanity or civil society—They never kept any company, but among themselves, and supported themselves wholly by robbing: being, moreover, so very cruel, that they never robbed anyone, whom they did not murder.

By this bloody method, and their being so retired from the world, they continued for a long time undiscovered, there being no person able to guess how the people were lost that went by the place where they lived. As soon as they had robbed any man, woman or child, they used to carry off the carcase to the den, where cutting it into quarters, they would pickle the mangled limbs, and afterwards eat it; this being their only sustenance: And notwithstanding, they were at last so numerous, they commonly had superfluity of this their abominable food, so that in the night time they frequently threw legs and arms of the unhappy wretches they had murdered into the sea, at a great distance from their bloody habitation: the limbs were often cast up by the tide in several parts of the country, to the astonishment and terror of all beholders, and others who heard of it.

Persons who have gone about their lawful occasions fell so often into their hands, that it caused a general outcry in the country round about: no person knowing what was become of their friends or relations, if they were once seen by these merciless cannibals.

All the people in the adjacent parts were at last alarmed at such an uncommon loss of their neighbours and acquaintances, for there was no travelling in safety near the den of these wretches: this occasioned spies to be frequently sent into these parts, many of whom never returned again, and those who did, after the strictest search and inquiry, could not find how these melancholy matters happened.

Several honest travellers were taken up on suspicion and wrongfully hanged upon bare circumstances: several innocent inn-keepers were executed, for no other reason than that persons, who had been thus lost, were known to have lain in their houses, which occasioned a suspicion of their being murdered by them, and their bodies privately buried in obscure places to prevent a discovery. Thus an illplaced justice was executed with the greatest severity imaginable, in order to prevent these frequent, atrocious deeds; so many innkeepers, who lived on the western road of Scotland, left their business, for fear of being made examples of, and followed other employments.

This, on the other hand, occasioned many inconveniences to travellers, who were now in great distress for accommodation when they were disposed to refresh themselves and horses, or take up lodging for the night. In a word, the whole country was almost depopulated.

Still the king's subjects were as much missed as before, so that it became the admiration of the whole kingdom how such villainies could be carried on, and the perpetrators not discovered. A great many had been executed, not one of them made any confession at the gallows, but maintained to the last, that they were perfectly innocent of the crime for which they suffered.

When the magistrates found all was in vain, they left off these rigorous proceedings, and trusted wholly to Providence, for the bringing to light the authors of these unparalleled barbarities when it should seem proper to the divine wisdom.

Sawney's family was at last grown very large, and every branch of it as soon as it was able, assisted in perpetrating their wicked deeds, which they still followed with impunity—Sometimes they would attack four, five or six, footmen together, but never more than two, if they were on horseback; they were, moreover, so careful, that not one whom they had set upon should escape, that an ambuscade was set on every side to secure them, let them fly which way they would, provided it should ever so happen that one or more got away from the first assailants. How was it possible they should be detected, when not one that saw them ever saw anybody else afterwards.

The place which they inhabited was quite solitary and lonesome, and, when the tide came up, the water went near two hundred yards into their subterraneous habitation, which reached almost a mile underground; so that when people, who have been sent armed to search all the places about, have passed by the mouth of the cave, they have never taken any notice of it, never supposing any human being would reside in such a place of perpetual horror and darkness.

The number of people these savages destroyed was never exactly known; but it was generally computed that in the twenty-five years they continued their butcheries, they had washed their hands in the blood of at least a thousand men, women and children. The manner they were at last discovered was as follows:

A man and his wife behind him on the same horse, coming one evening home from a fair, and falling into the ambuscade of these merciless wretches, they fell upon them in a furious manner. The man to save himself as well as he could, fought very bravely against them with sword and pistol, riding some of them down by main force of his horse.

In the conflict the poor woman fell from behind him, and was instantly butchered before her husband's face, for the female cannibals cut her throat, and fell to sucking her blood with as great a gust, as if it had been wine: this done, they ript up her belly, and pulled out her entrails. Such a dreadful spectacle made the man make the more obstinate resistance, as he expected the same fate, if he fell into their hands.

It pleased Providence while he was engaged that twenty or thirty who had been at the same fair, came together in a body; upon which Sawney Bean and his bloodthirsty clan withdrew and, made the best of their way through a thick wood to their den.

This man who was the first who had ever fell in their way, and came off alive, told the whole company what had happened, and shewed them the horrid spectacle of his wife, whom the murderers had dragged to some distance, but had not time to carry her entirely off. They were all struck with stupefaction and amazement at what he related: they took him with them to Glasgow, and told the affair to the magistrates of that city, who immediately sent to the King concerning it.

In about three or four days after, his majesty in person, with a body of about four hundred men set out for the place where this dismal tragedy was acted, in order to search all the rocks and thickets, that, if possible, they might apprehend this hellish crew, which had been so long pernicious to all the western parts of the kingdom.

The man who was attacked was the guide, and care was taken to have a large number of bloodhounds with them, that no human means might be wanting towards their putting an entire end to these cruelties.

No sign of any habitation was to be found for a long time; and even when they came to the wretches' cave they took no notice of it, but were going to pursue their search along the sea shore, the tide being then out; but some of the bloodhounds luckily entered the Cimmerian den, and instantly set up a most hideous barking, howling and yelping; so that the king, with his attendants, came back, and looked into it: they could not tell how to conceive that any thing human could be concealed in a place where they saw nothing but darkness; nevertheless, as the blood-hounds increased their noise they went farther in, and refused to come back again; they then began to imagine something or other must inhabit there. Torches were immediately sent for, and a great many men ventured in, through the most intricate turnings and windings, till at last they arrived at that private recess from all the world, which was the habitation of these monsters.

Now the whole body, or as many of them as could went in, and were all so shocked at what they beheld, that they were almost ready to sink into the earth. Legs, arms, thighs, hands and feet of men, women and children, were hung up in rows, like dried beef; a great many limbs laid in pickle, and a great mass of money both gold and silver, with watches, rings, swords, pistols and a large quantity of clothes, both linen and woollen, and an infinite number of other things which they had taken from those they had murdered, were thrown together in heaps or hung up against the sides of the den.

Sawney's family, at this time, besides himself, consisted of his wife, eight sons, six daughters, eighteen grandsons, and fourteen grand-daughters, who were all begotten in incest.

These were all seized and pinioned by his majesty's order in the first place: then they took what human flesh they could find, and buried it in the sands: afterwards loading themselves with the spoils which they found, they returned to Edinburgh with their prisoners; all the country, as they passed along, flocked to see this cursed tribe. When they came to their journey's end, the wretches were committed to the Tolbooth, from whence they were next day conducted, under a strong guard to Leith, where they were executed without any process, it being thought needless to try creatures who were even professed enemies of mankind.

The men were dismembered, their hands and legs were severed from their bodies, by which amputation they bled to death in a few hours. The wife, daughters and grand-children having been made spectators of this just punishment inflicted on the men, were afterwards burnt to death in three several fires. They all in general died without the least signs of repentance, but continued cursing and venting the most dreadful imprecations to the very last gasp of life.

2

The Legend in Literature

A being, whom no blessed word,
To ghostly peace can bring;
A wretch, at whose approach abhor'd
Recoils each holy thing.

SIR WALTER SCOTT, *The Gray Brother*

The *Legend of Sawney Bean* was first printed in the form of a broadsheet about the year 1700, which was a very significant time in the history of printing and publishing in Britain. Although the printing press had been active for about two hundred years before that time the number of books published was low, partially because of high costs, but mainly because of the low level of literacy among the people.

The literacy level began to rise at the end of the seventeenth century and produced a reading audience which could be satisfied by printing and selling broadsheets, or broadsides, on a geographically local basis. The centres of literacy did not seem to coincide with the centres of population. As Boswell mentions in his *Life of Johnson*, there were no bookshops in Birmingham in 1709 and Johnson's father, whose bookshop was at Lichfield, used to have a temporary shop there on market days.

A typical broadsheet would consist of a single large sheet of paper with four pages of a book printed on each side of it, the purchaser would then fold and cut it to make a booklet. Thus there were no binding or bookmaking costs and the printing procedures were cut to a minimum. The first page was cover, title page and advertising matter in one, which explains the long, descriptive and provocative titles. Some of the more expensive broadsheets carried more pages and were embellished with woodcuts depicting persons or scenes connected with the subject matter.

Sawney Bean and Dick Turpin the Highwayman are the only two characters introduced to the popular press at that time which are still well known today and have not lost their original attraction during the two centuries which have intervened.

The author's researches have discovered only four broadsheets on the subject of Sawney Bean, all of which can be seen at the National Library of Scotland, in Edinburgh.

The Horrid Life of Sawney Beane. An Atrocious Robber & Assassin. Printed by Jollie and Sons, Carlisle. (8 pp.)

The History of Sawney Beane and His Family; Robbers and Murderers. Printed and Sold in Aldermary Church Yard. London. (8 pp. 5 Cuts.)

The Life of Sawney Beane, The Man-Eater, Who inhabited a Cave near the Sea-Side in the County of Galloway in Scotland, upwards of Twenty-Five Years. To Which is Added The Droll Jester, Or Laugh when you can.
J. Ferraby, Printer, Butchery, Hull. (23 pp.)

The fourth is identical to the above except that Ferraby's address is given as *Market Place, Hull.* None of these give the date of printing nor any indication of how many editions had preceded it, so that it is only possible to say with absolute certainty that they existed before the next phase in printing and publishing which can be dated with accuracy.

The subject matter of broadsheets in general was of a bloody and violent nature, and it was just as popular with the more well-to-do reader as the commoner. They dealt with the lives of murderers and highwaymen, incidents in battles, traitorous plots and similar topics. In short, they were the forerunners of the more lurid newspapers of today. For the more wealthy readers, especially those in London and other large cities, printers found it profitable to bind the subject matter of a number of broadsheets between hard-backs with the addition of larger pages and better and clearer print. The two most popular of these books, and the forerunner of the long-lived series of *Newgate Calendars*, were:

A Compleat History of the Lives and Robberies of the most Notorious Highway-men, Foot-pads, Shop-lifters, and Cheats of both sexes, in and about London and Westminster, and all parts of Great Britain, for above an Hundred Years past, continued to the present time. The Fifth Edition (adorn'd with Cuts). By Captain Alexander Smith. London 1719.

And

A General and True History of the Lives and Actions of the most Famous Highwaymen, Murderers, Street-Robbers, etc. To which is added a genuine Account of the Voyages and Plunders of the most Noted Pirates, Interspersed with Several Remarkable Tryals of the most Notorious Malefactors, at the Sessions-House in the Old Baily, London. Adorn'd with the Effigies, and other material Transactions of the most remarkable Offenders, engraved on copper-plates. By Capt. Charles Johnson. London 1734.

There was an identical edition marked Birmingham 1742 but there is the possibility that the London edition was printed in Birmingham. Boswell remarked upon a book translated by Samuel Johnson which "was published in 1735 with London upon the title-page, though it was in reality printed in Birmingham, a device too common with provincial publishers", and this seems to indicate that London was not quite so important in the publishing field at that time as may be supposed.

Both of these books were collections of broadsheets which had already been circulating for some time and when their contents are compared it is seen that Johnson had mainly copied the material already used by Smith with some new additions. Part of this new material was the *Legend of Sawney Bean*, which provides the latest possible date of his introduction into literature. His absence from the Smith material does not prove conclusively that broadsheets of his story did not exist before 1719, but it does indicate the unlikelihood of their existing in the previous century.

The legend then became enshrined in the *Newgate Calendars* and not a single word of it was changed throughout the various printings, except for the mis-printing of Galloway as Oalgay in *The History of Sawney Beane* broadsheet, until 1843.

At this time the production of books and printing matter in general in Britain stood at the cross-roads. As a result of the Industrial Revolution it was about to take a step forward in a way never before possible and Sawney Bean was about to be swept forward with it.

The dramatic increase in the number of books published in the latter half of the nineteenth century was mainly due to the increase in literacy of the population at large and to the technical improvements in book production. In the ten years between 1820 and 1830 impetus was given to the publishing industry by the introduction of machine-manufactured paper and the rotary steam press.

Archibald Constable had foreseen this in 1825 when he announced his plan to create a publishing empire (Sir Walter Scott said he would become "the great Napoleon of the realms of print"), but he found himself bankrupt within two years because he had misjudged the situation and was too soon in the field. With the cost of paper halved and the speed of printing increased, after about 1840 books were available at a reasonably low price to a public eager to read them.

Sawney Bean returned to his native Galloway when the legend was printed by John Nicholson at Kirkcudbright in a collection entitled *Historical and Traditional Tales connected with the South of Scotland* in 1843. This version, which is reproduced as the first chapter of this book, differs in certain ways from the previous versions mentioned and became the new standard version from that date.

Firstly, there were minor alterations which clarified and updated the use of words to make reading easier. Some of these were from "took up their habitation in a rock" to "in a cave"; and from "to bait themselves and horses, or put up lodging at the night" to "refresh themselves and horses, or take up lodging for the night". This is good editorial practice and is certainly in order since two hundred years had elapsed since the first writing.

His second set of changes were probably out of respect for the Victorian predjudices of his readers, for he toned-down the forthright language of the original by changing "this hellish cur" to "this hellish crew" and by completely omitting half of the first sentence of the final paragraph. This originally read, "The Men had first their Privy-Members cut off, and thrown into the Fire before their Faces, and their Hands and Legs were severed from their Bodies; by which Amputations they bled to Death in some Hours."

However, his most important change was to replace "Sawney Beane was born . . . sometime in the reign of Queen Elizabeth while James 1st governed Scotland" to "in the reign of James I of Scotland". There seems to be no good reason for this change unless Nicholson possessed some local traditional knowledge which prompted him to move the story back in time some two hundred years, thus correcting an error made by the English publishers who had become confused by their being two Jameses, who could be called "the first". Whether or not this was intentional, it created confusion in later years and will bear closer examination in a later chapter.

The overall effect was to change the image of Sawney from a depraved criminal who had been executed less than a hundred years before the first printing, to a legendary figure who was said to have existed about four hundred years before the Nicholson version. Perhaps he was setting the record to rights, but the horrifying activities of the Bean Clan were such that they were not to be allowed to sink back into the legendary past. British publishing was about to enter a new phase and Sawney the cannibal was to take his rightful place in the literature of horror.

This was the age of Dickens, the Brontës and Thackeray; the age when the English Novel blossomed and through its interaction with its readers brought about great social changes. But, at the same time, the steadily growing reading public was avid for entertainment, wonders, thrills and excitement. There were literally millions of copies of *Maria Marten or the Murder in the Red Barn*[1] printed and sold after this date. Gothic chillers of varying literary status, including *Frankenstein*, and *The Castle of Otranto*, appeared and authors such as Sir Walter Scott and W. H. Ainsworth produced large numbers of books with a bias towards horror. Even Dickens tried his hand in this field just before his death, which prevented the completion of *The Mystery of Edwin Drood*.

Sawney Bean was a character ready-made for this aspect of the Novel and Thomas Preskett Prest was the ideal author to make the most of his gory reputation. Prest was noted for his novels (sometimes of almost a thousand pages and over two hundred chapters) which dwelt at length on every aspect of horror. His most enduring work was *Sweeny Tod, the Demon Barber of Fleet Street*, but *Varney the Vampire* (published 1874) was so popular that it was again published in serial form six years later and a sequel followed entitled *The Monk and Varney*.

Prest was prolific. The year 1844 saw the publication of *The Black Monk or The Secret of the Grey Turret*, *The Death Grasp or A Father's Curse* and *The Maniac Father or The Victim of Seduction*. This gives some idea of the small amount of time he had to spare, or was inclined to spare, on researching facts.

In the event, Prest's *Sawney Bean; the Man-Eater of Midlothian* added nothing to the status of the legend. The story he produced might be described as a long, rambling Victorian romance by the present-day reader; and it had very little to do with the traditional content of the legend except, of course, for the leading characters and was set in the country about Edinburgh.

What he did do was to publicise the legend to the extent that there was little danger of it ever being lost. He also added flesh to the bare bones of the account he must have found in Captain Johnson's book by using his imagination to furnish the two-dimensional figure of Sawney Bean he found there with thoughts, feelings, emotions and everyday actions which made him seem alive.

It may reasonably be supposed that Gilbert and Sullivan satirised this author, or at least this literary genre, in their comic-opera *Ruddigore or the Witch's Curse* in 1887. To have been the success it certainly was, the subject matter and its implications and absurdities must have been understood and appreciated by a very wide section of the population; which is further evidence of how widely these books were read.

In 1896, about fifty years after the Prest version, the Bean Clan appeared in S. R. Crockett's *The Grey Man*. Crockett was a Galwegian, born in 1859 at Laurieston Village, and well versed in the traditions and folk-lore of his own region which prompted him to introduce details which caused his books to ring with authority. At times he was inclined to introduce inaccuracies and exaggerations to enhance the romantic aspects of his works but, as we shall see, even the exaggerations seem to be part of the traditions of Galloway.

Nevertheless, it was his detailed knowledge of the history of the region, or his access to a fund of local oral tradition, which made Sawney Bean, although a secondary character in *The Grey Man*, into a three dimensional figure. He improved immeasurably upon the legend without changing the basic structure and brought it to life.

This novel had fifty-two chapters and 358 pages. Perhaps this fell a little short of the average Prest volume, and the title could be considered modest by comparison. However, what it lacked in this direction it made up for in the chapter headings. A few of these were "The Ogre's Castle", "The Cave of Death", "The Werewolf of Benerard" and "The Place of the Legion of Devils". It was set in the year 1580 in the reign of James the Sixth; so it did not depart from the original version on this score as the Nicholson version had.

The literary versions of the legend reached their peak with Crockett's work. It not only portrayed a well-rounded set of characters, but revealed the value of the source references from which it was drawn. The following short passages are selected to illustrate these points and will be discussed further in a later chapter.

Marjorie and Nell Kennedy, together with Launce, the narrator, and the Dominie, or Schoolmaster, have been surprised in the cave and have hidden from sight to watch events.

> Then I knew that these execrable hell-hounds must be the hideous crew who called Sawney Bean lord and master. They were of both sexes and all ages, mostly running naked, the more stalwart of them armed with knives and whingers, or with knotted pieces of tree in which a ragged stone had been thrust and tied with sinew or tags of rope. The very tottering children were striking at one another, or biting like wolves, till the blood flowed. In the corner sat an old bleared hag, who seemed of some authority over them, for she pointed with her finger, and the

uproar calmed itself a little. The shameless naked women-crew began to bestir themselves, and heaped broken driftwood upon the floor, to which presently a light was set....

The cavern was very high in the midst, but the sides not so high—rather like the sloping roof of an attic which slants quickly down from the rooftree. But that which took my eye amid the smoke were certain vague shapes, as it had been the limbs of human beings, shrunk and blackened, which hung in rows on either side of the cave. At first it seemed that my eyes must certainly deceive me, for the reek drifted hither and thither, and made the rheum flow from them with its bitterness. But after a little study of these wall adornments, I could make nothing else of it, than that these poor relics, which hung in rows from the roof of the cave like hams and black puddings set to dry in the smoke, were indeed no other than the parched arms and legs of men and women, who had once walked upon the upper earth—but by misfortune had fallen into the power of this hideous, inconceivable gang of monstrous man-eaters....

But there was that nearer to me which smote me down like a blow taking a man unawares. As I stood up to look, gripping nervously at my sword and peering over, there came a gust off the sea, roaring up the passages of the cavern. For with the moon the wind had risen without. The fire on the floor flickered upward and filled the place with light. I felt something touch my cheek. Speedily I turned, and, lo! it was a little babe's hand that swung by a cord. The wind had caught it, so light it was, and it had rubbed my cheek.

After a while a sound was heard in the passageway and the dark shadow of a huge, bent man appeared in the doorway.

The monster stood a moment in the doorway as though angered at something, then he spoke in a voice like a beast's growl, certain things which I could not at all understand—though it was clear that his progeny did, for there ensued a tumultuous rushing from side to side. Then Sawney Bean strode into the midst of his den. It happened that by misadventure he stumbled and set his foot upon a lad of six or seven, judging by the size of him, who sprawled naked in the doorway. The imp squirmed round like a serpent and bit Sawney Bean in the leg, whereat he stooped, and catching the lad by the feet, he dashed his head with a dull crash against the wall, and threw him quivering like a dead rabbit into the corner.

> The rest stood for a moment aghast. But in a trice, and without a single one so much as going to see if the boy was dead or only stunned, the whole hornet's byke hummed again, and the place was filled with a stifling smell of burning fat and roasting victual, upon the origin of which I dared not let my mind for a moment dwell.

Sawney then approached the corner in which they were hidden. Discovery being inevitable and escape impossible, the men decided to kill the girls themselves rather than allow them to fall into the hands of the cannibals; then fight to the death taking as many as possible with them.

> I heard the beast-man's step on the stair. I looked from Nell's dear neck to her eyes and back again to her bosom. Then I lifted my hand with the steel in it, and nerved myself for the striking, for I must make no mistake. And even in that moment I saw the gleam of a dagger in Marjorie's hand also.
>
> Suddenly a tremendous rush of sound filled the cave. The blade fell from my hand, and by instinct, not knowing what we did, Nell and I clasped one another. The clamour seemed to be about us and all around us. Roaring echos came back to us. The bowels of the earth quaked. Yet methought there was something strongly familiar in the sound of it. I turned me about, and there, standing erect with all his little height was the Dominie. His cheeks were distended, and he was blowing upon his great war-pipes such a thunderous pibroch as had never been heard east of the Minch since the island pipes skirled on the Red Harlaw.
>
> The pack of fiends that caroused and slew beneath, stood stricken a moment in amaze at the dreadful, incomprehensible sounds. Then they fled helter-skelter, yellyhooing with fear, down the narrow sea-way from which the tide had now fully ebbed. And when I looked again, there was not a soul to be seen. Only over the edge of a lappered cauldron the body of the murdered woman (or, at least, a part of it), lay doubled—bloody incentive to make haste out of this direful Cave of Death.

After this magnificent portrayal by Crockett there was no new attempt to re-interpret the Sawney Bean legend for another eighty years. In the meantime the Nicholson version became the "standard". Dorothy L. Sayers published it in *Detection, Mystery & Horror. Part 2.* which first appeared in 1928 and was repeatedly republished until the late 1940s, thus keeping it before the eyes of the public.

At the same time some attempt was made to present the legend in a fresh light by paraphrasing it. J. J. Bell, in *The Glory of Scotland* (1932), paraphrased the Nicholson version into a much shorter and lighter account suitable for inclusion in a travel-book for general reading. He writes of the cave:

> But it was more than that; it was a larder. On the rocky walls were plenteous supplies of food, in the shape of human limbs, smoked or pickled in brine. For, you see, Mr Bean and his large family were cannibals. . . .

Two years later Sawney was again receiving the attention of the Law in the shape of William Roughead, a noted authority on criminal trials, who produced a book giving accounts of nine notable murderers, three English and six Scottish—including Sawney Bean. Roughead was working from the Birmingham edition of Captain Johnson's book, from which he accepted James the Sixth just as Bell had accepted James the First from Nicholson. In fact, he did more than merely accept James the Sixth; he considered that James and Sawney were so alike in their own particular ways that a little dry cynicism was in order.

> In the golden age of good King James, Sixth of Scotland, and First of England, under whose benificent sway, in terms of the Prayer for those who are set in authority over us, peace and happiness, truth and justice, religion and piety were established among us for all generations; in those palmy days, I say, there dwelt with his fertile spouse and formidable progeny, upon the sea coast of the west country, near Ballantrae in Carrick, one Mr Alexander, more familiarly Sawney, Beane. This gentleman was every way worthy to be the subject of so enlightened a monarch. He was homely and unconventional in his domestic habits; he lived largely, as we shall see, upon his fellow men; and his respect for the law of self-preservation was greater than that which he paid to the moral code commonly attributed to Moses.[2]

Here, for the first time on record, was mentioned the traditional location of Sawney Bean's cave—apart from a vague indication by Crockett. This is a purely oral tradition which sites the cave under Bennane Head, about three miles north of Ballantrae. There is nothing on record to support this assertion, but a later chapter will be devoted to a search for the cave and its probable location.

1967 saw the next paraphrase in C. E. Maine's *The Worlds Strangest Crimes*, in which he commented on twenty unusual crimes and criminals including Sawney Bean, which was probably suggested by a recent paper-back of the *Newgate Calendar* which carried the Johnson version.

At this time, when interest in the legend seemed to be lower than it had ever been before, forces were at work which were to change the situation again. In Edinburgh—the scene of his supposed execution—Sawney returned to public prominence and acclaim when the play, *Sawney Bean*, was performed at the Edinburgh Festival of 1969. The legend had taken another step forward and a new lease of life in a different media.

Because the play is outside the scope of this chapter, and as it brings the situation up to date, it is considered more suitable that the play be dealt with separately in the final chapter of the book.

3

How do Legends begin?

> To learn it we have tradition; namely, that so we believe, because both we from our predecessors, and they from theirs have so received.
>
> HOOKER

Although stated to be "as well attested as any historical fact can be", no supporting documents have yet come to light to confirm the existence of Sawney Bean. The same is true of the valiant Dick Turpin and his celebrated horse Black Bess although Captain Johnson presented them both in the same book, together with many others, as well-known criminals of the day. They both became legendary figures and joined that famous company which includes Robin Hood and William Tell.

Fame in itself, even after several hundred years, is not necessarily proof of existence; and even if existence is proved there may possibly be a wide discrepancy between the fact and the legend. The great problem in seeking a solution to these difficulties lies in the fact that very few records were made in earlier times and these mainly excluded the ordinary people of the land. Apart from his plays, how little we really know about the life of Shakespeare.

This was particularly true of Scotland and was commented upon in 1824 by a writer of Galloway:

> Yet for all, till of late, the Scotch peasantry have been allowed to remain in their dear rural mountains and dales,

without being ever looked at almost by travellers, or said a word about by historians. It was not until they themselves found out the way of noting upon paper, that anything respecting them has come to light; and their great modesty hath not allowed them even yet to say very much.

We have volumes on volumes, as many as would fill a score of wheel-barrows, all wrote respecting our Kings, Queens and *ither big fowk*, yet hardly a word said about the people; nor is this neglect to be wondered at, when we consider what stir these nobles made in the days of yore; no poor penman chap durst think or speak of any other creature but them. . . .

So then, our works in the vernacular language of the olden times are but scanty; and suppose there had been more, suppose there had been yet extant the poems of fifty bards as old as Tom the Rymer or Barbour, still I am inclined to think that the lingo of those distant days, as spoken by the peasantry, could not be hunted out; the natives mostly of every nation, have generally at least two tongues they work with, the rustic and the polite, the one spoken by the grandees, the other by the commonality; now, methinks, our old bards have all written in the former, for it is the same language with ancient English and German, in their day: for my own part, I doubt there has ever been a genuine rustic manuscript of an ancient date come before the world.[3]

Amusingly put, perhaps, but absolutely true. Before the seventeenth century very few people could read and fewer books existed. Knowledge, information and tales were handed down by an oral tradition. Grandfather would sit in the winter firelight telling the stories that his grandfather had told him. The amount of knowledge stored and passed on in this way must have been considerable for the human brain can hold more information than the best computer produced today. Indeed, the human race has only survived because it was able to pass on the wealth of experience gained from trial and error, bitter experences and successes, from generation to generation with accuracy.

Information on the practical arts could be reinforced by demonstration and practice; but the transmission of philosophy, history, news, religious teachings and other non-demonstrable arts was another matter. The tellers of tales and singers of ballads strove diligently to become word-perfect in conveying the message of their story with accuracy. Nevertheless all stories and legends were originally coined with a purpose in view—to praise a hero, decry a villain or to point a moral—and certain aspects of it were coloured either to enhance the purpose or simply to make the tale more entertaining. Surprising examples of how the basic accuracy of a legend has been maintained over many centuries can be quoted.

There was a pre-historic (Celtic) burial-mound, known locally as *Bryn-yr-ellyon* or The Hill of the Fairies, near the village of Mold in Flintshire which was removed (not excavated) in 1832. "It was believed in the country around to be haunted by a spectre in golden armour. When more than three hundred loads of stones had been carted away, the workmen came to the skeleton of a tall and powerful man placed at full length. He had been laid there in a finely wrought corselet of gold, with a lining of bronze: the former was found to be a thin plate of the precious metal measuring three feet seven inches long by eight inches wide." After it had been removed to the British Museum, the stories of the spectre no longer circulated. There is no alternative for us but to accept that the story of the burial had been handed down from generation to generation for at least fifteen hundred years. It had changed in form during that time, but the basic facts had remained.[4]

In Scotland, a very similar tale was told of a mound in Fife which was supposed to be haunted by a warrior in silver armour. Local men had secretly dug into it in 1819 and the truth was brought to light when they tried to sell the silver to a silversmith in Cupar.

In the light of this information it would be wrong to dismiss the Sawney Bean legend, or any other folk-tale, without first testing the possibility of its antiquity and accuracy. Methods of attempting this have been developed over the last century.

Before about the year 1800 there was very little interest in the study of folk-tales in Britain. They were considered to be stories for children or simple people and of no great depth or importance. But with the printing of *Household Tales* by the Brothers Grimm in 1812 and John Brand's *Observations on Popular Antiquities* in England in 1813, interest increased rapidly. The term 'folk-lore' was coined by W. J. Thoms in 1846 and the Folk-lore Society was formed in 1878. During this century folk-lore became a very popular subject, and almost every parson and his wife set about collecting and committing to paper the myths, fairy tales and legends of their own parishes and districts.

The Scottish reference volumes entitled the *Statistical Report* were compiled by clerics in just this way and references will be made to them later.

After collecting came analysis when it began to be obvious that not only were there similarities between folk-tales on the national level, but on the international level as well. The folk-tales of Scotland and Ireland (but not so much England) had much in common with those of Norway, Germany and other European countries. The realisation that certain aspects could be traced back to the common basis of the Celtic religion was to come later.

This scientific approach of cross-referencing was first taken by Sabine Baring-Gould, a clergyman and eminent folk-lorist, about 1870 when he introduced the idea of "story radicals" or themes which would be seen to be common in stories from many countries. He explained his idea as follows:

> Every language had its primary roots, and these roots united together, expanded, somewhat altered with wear-and-tear, became words. The number of radices is fixed. It is small; the words formed from them were innumerable and continually changing. There was a root in primeval Aryan languages which had the signification of enclosing, it was probably *g* (vowel) *rd*. From this root we have a garden, a garth, a yard; to gird, a girdle; a ward, either one kept enclosed or an enclosure, of which the keeper is a warden; and a measure of land to be enclosed is a yard. . . .
>
> In all cognate languages we find the same roots which, however much altered, can be identified and reduced to their primitive form.
>
> Much the same may be said of household tales. In all nations belonging to the same stock there exists stories resembling each other in many particulars, and differing from each other in others; yet with an unmistakable radical unity about them, which makes it easy to reduce them to a primeval root. . . . Sometimes in the same nation one radical has developed into several distinct ideas; as garden and warden: so with stories, they may not resemble each other in much that is superficial, yet a critical eye can often perceive their radical identity.

The following example gives his themes for *Jack the Giant Killer*.

Section 111. Men in conflict with supernatural beings.
A. Men obtain the Mastery by Cunning.
1. Jack the Giant Killer root.
1. A man is matched with giants or devils.
2. He deceives them by his superior cunning.
3. He makes them kill themselves.

From this beginning others took up the work of codifying folk-tale themes. A comprehensive system was produced by Stith Thompson in *Motif-Index of Folk Literature* which was published in six volumes between 1955 and 1958 and contained several thousand themes or motifs. Some examples of these are printed below.

Motif No.	*Section D* *Magic*
D1318.5.2.	Corpse bleeds when murderer touches it.
D1810.8.3.2.	Dream warns of danger which will happen in near future.
	Section E *The Dead*
E422.1.1.4.	Headless ghost carries head under arm.
E581.2.	Ghost rides horse.
E723.	Wraiths of persons separate from body.
	Section F *Marvels*
F211.2.	Fairyland entrance under stones.
F531.3.2.	Giant throws rock.
	Section G *Ogres*
G61.	Relatives' flesh eaten unwittingly.
G243.	Witches' sabbath.
G303.9.1.1.	Devil as builder of bridge.

In 1961 Thompson, aided by Antti Aarne, produced a work on the main themes of folk-tales entitled *The Types of the Folk-tale* which codified them in the following way:

Types	300– 749.	Tales of Magic.
Types	750– 849.	Religious Tales.
Types	850– 999.	Romantic Tales.
Types	1000–1199.	Tales of the Stupid Ogre.
Types	1200–1999.	Jokes and Anecdotes.

By this system, for example, the famous tale of *Rumpelstilskin* can be reduced and codified as follows.

Type	500.	The Names of the Helper.
Motif	H521.	Test: guessing unknown propounders name.
Motif	H1092.	Tasks: spinning impossible amount in one night.
Motif	N475.	Secret name overheard by eavesdropper.

This particular story has many versions in practically every country in Europe, but Ireland, Finland, Germany and Denmark seem to have more than any other.

This century of valuable work inter-related the themes of legends as they are known *at this time*. They do not attempt to trace them back to their origins, but it is perfectly clear that many tales are of great age and have travelled about Europe with the migrations of people over the centuries; changing in detail, but never in basics, as they were passed from generation to generation.

It is the purpose of this book to attempt to trace the origins of the legend of Sawney Bean using as many techniques and sources of information as possible and in this chapter we shall compare it with another legend. The English traditional tale most similar to that of Sawney Bean is "Bloody Baker" which, by other of its themes, can be associated with the tales of "Mr Fox" and "Bluebeard".

THE LEGEND OF BLOODY BAKER

Bloody Baker, returning from abroad with a foreign servant, took up his abode in an old house near Cranbrook in Kent. Soon stories were heard of cries coming from the house at night, of robberies in the nearby woods and of travellers who were never heard of again. Baker had been penniless before he left England, but now he began to purchase more and more property. At last he began to pay attentions to a rich young lady of the district who often wore valuable jewellery and sometimes urged her to visit his house to see the strange objects he had brought back from abroad.

The lady always refused his invitations, but being in the neighbourhood one day in the company of an older lady decided to pay him an unannounced visit. Her friend tried to persuade her otherwise, but she knocked on the door and, as there was no reply, entered and began to explore. On the staircase was a parrot cage containing a parrot which cried out:

"Peep O! pretty lady! be not too bold,
Or your red blood will soon run cold!"

Which it did, for the first door she opened revealed a room full of the bodies of murdered women. Hearing a noise outside they espied through the window Bloody Baker and his servant bringing in yet another body and, trembling with fear, concealed themselves under the staircase.

The door opened and the two men were carrying the corpse close by their hiding place when its hand caught between the railings and almost caused them to drop it. With an oath Baker severed the hand with his dagger and it fell into the lap of one of the ladies below. At the first opportunity they fled carrying the hand with them, which bore a ring upon the finger. Information was given to the constables and the people who had lost relatives and a trap was prepared for Baker.

The lady invited Baker to a party, to which he came without suspicion, during which the lady told her tale to the company presenting it as a terrible dream. "Fair lady," said Baker, "dreams are nothing; they are but fables."

"Is this a fable?" she replied displaying the severed hand. Before he could escape the constables appeared and arrested him. He was punished by being burned alive, the tradition states, although the Queen tried to save him on account of his religion.

This comparison leads to a number of interesting conclusions. As has already been indicated, this tale is similar—indeed almost identical—with the story of "Mr Fox", except that during the recounting of the dream Mr Fox repeats a phrase several times. "It is not so, nor it was not so, And God forbid it should be so!"

It seems that the story of "Mr Fox" was well known at the time of Shakespeare, for it appears to be the source of a line in *Much Ado About Nothing* when, in Act 1, Scene 1, Benedick says "Like the old tale, my Lord; it is not so, nor 'twas not so, but indeed, God forbid it should be so." This play was first produced in 1598 which suggests that the Queen mentioned in the Bloody Baker version was either Elizabeth I or "Bloody" Mary who preceded her.

On investigation we find that Sir John Baker was Chancellor of the Exchequer to "Bloody" Mary, the Catholic Queen, and, like her, was noted for his persecution of Protestants—particularly Anabaptists who were numerous in Kent. He was not burned, but died peacefully at his house in London in 1558.

It might be concluded from the dates mentioned that "Bloody Baker" is older than "Mr Fox", but further consideration makes it obvious that "Mr Fox" is older and that "Bloody Baker" was a special version of "Mr Fox" locally coined in Kent to perpetuate the religious hatred for Sir John Baker. Only this could account for "Bloody Baker" receiving poetic justice by being burned to death in place of the real John Baker who, with his Queen, had been responsible for the mass burning of Protestants during her reign. Hanging, not burning, was the legal punishment for murder at that time—burning was reserved for heretics and religious dissenters.

This shows how legends change with the passing of time. Religious beliefs and religious propaganda has had a profound effect on household tales and folk-beliefs which has lasted for many centuries and this must be taken into account when they are considered.

According to Höffding's *Philosophy of Religion*, "In a Danish village church the custom of bowing when passing a certain spot in the church wall was maintained into the nineteenth century, but no one knew the reason for this, until, on the white-wash being scraped away, a picture of the Madonna was found on the wall: thus the custom had outlived the Catholicism which prompted it by three hundred years."

Political influences often have the same effect of retaining a tradition after the original purpose has been lost, and this must also be taken into account.

It was a custom of all classes of people in Edinburgh, during the late eighteenth century, to touch their hats respectfully when passing the Cross in the High Street, although nobody seemed to know why. On hearing that the Disarming Act had been repealed, the Rev. Robert MacGregor, the first minister of the Gaelic Chapel of Edinburgh, marched to the Cross dressed in full Highland dress, which had hitherto been forbidden, at the head of a large gathering of Scots. He merely held an informal service, but the crowd became so large that the authorities thought it wise to have the Town Guard clear them away.

It can only be supposed that this was an association of ideas, for it was at the Cross that the Standards of all the clans which were defeated at Culloden were burned after the '45 rebellion. A procession descended from the Castle, first the hangman with the Pretender's Colours then a line of chimney-sweeps carrying the others, and threw them onto the fire.

The comparison shows that Sawney Bean and Bloody Baker have a number of aspects in common; the corpses, the riches obtained from them, the missing travellers, death by burning and the intervention of the monarch. Bloody Baker and Mr Fox can be traced back to 1550 without difficulty, one hundred and fifty years before Sawney Bean saw print. It is possible that they originated from a common stock.

Apparently Bloody Baker was not a cannibal; yet he stored the corpses. There is an inconsistency here which suggests that this aspect was dropped during the period before the tale was "collected" in the nineteenth century—or else the listener was supposed to take it for granted.

Unfortunately, Scotland had no equivalent to Shakespeare to hint at the existence of Sawney Bean; nor was he among the ranks of *ither big fowk*, as was Sir John Baker, which would have ensured a cross-reference to a historical document. However, a part of the pattern has been established and we must now turn to other methods of investigation.

4

Ogres, Fairies and Ghosts

All nations have their omens drear,
Their legends wild of woe and fear,
To Cambria look—the peasant see,
Bethinks him of Glendowerdy,
And shun the Spirit's Blasted Tree.

SIR WALTER SCOTT, *Marmion*

Practically everything that has been said about folk-tales may also be said about ballads for these were handed down in the same manner. The ballad served the same purpose with the addition that it was sometimes a work-song sung to the rhythm of, say, the spinning-wheel or loom.

One book of importance in this field is *The English and Scottish Popular Ballads* edited by Francis James Child and published in five volumes between 1882 and 1898. In these were printed no less than twenty eight versions of the ballad "Mary Hamilton", twenty seven of "The Twa Sisters" and twenty five of "Lord Randal" with variations found in Italy, Germany, France, Iceland and other countries.

Robin Hood first appeared in ballad form; and we may be surprised to find that the Swiss outlaw, William Tell, had an English counterpart in the ballad "Adam Bell, Clim the Clough and William of Cloudesly".

And bound therto his eldest sonne,
And bad hym stande styll thereat,
And turned the childes face fro him,
Because he shud not sterte.

An apple upon his head he set,
And then his bowe he bent;
Syxe score paces they were outmet,
And thither Cloudesle went.

There he drew out a fayre brode arrowe;
Hys bowe was great and longe;
He set the arrowe in his bow,
That was both styffe and strong.

He prayed the people that was there
That they would styll stande;
For he that shooteth for such a wager,
Behoveth a steadfast hand.

Muche people prayed foe Cloudesle,
That hys life saved myght be,
And whan he made hym redy to shote,
There was many a weepynge eye.

Thus Clowdesle clefte the apple in two,
That many a man it se;
"Ouer goddes forbode," sayd the kynge,
"That thou sholdest shote at me!"

This ballad dates back to about 1550 in a written English version but the main theme, since it can be found in the Norse, German and other traditions, is certainly of much earlier origin.

Surely the most arresting example of the continued accuracy of the legend is the discovery of the city of Troy through the epic-poems of Homer, written about 850 B.C. As Robert Silverberg succinctly put it, "Homer has always been read. But, until the nineteenth century—until the coming of a monomaniac named Schliemann, in fact—no-one regarded the *Iliad* and the *Odyssey* as anything more colourful than tale-spinning. The city of Troy? A myth."

Heinrich Schliemann was born in 1822 in Mecklenburg (later part of the German Empire) of poor parents. His father was a pastor, so interested in ancient history that he fired Heinrich's imagination by reading the *Iliad* and *Odyssey*. This keen interest and determination that he would one day find the city of Troy stayed with him through the years he spent rising from an errand-boy to a banker in spite of the general opinion that it did not exist.

Thomas Bulfinch, a professor at Harvard College, reflected popular opinion in his *The Age of Fable* (1855). "The prevailing opinion of the learned, at this time, seems to be that the framework and much of the structure of the poems belongs to Homer, but that there are numerous interpolations and additions by other hands. . . . Virgil (on the other hand) is far inferior to Homer in originality and invention, but superior to him in correctness and elegance."

In 1863 Schliemann decided he had enough money to finance his own archaeological expedition, sold his business and set out for Turkey. Relying entirely upon the accuracy of Homer, he discarded the possibility of the village of Bounarbashi, favourable though it seemed from other aspects, because it did not lie near the sea and was situated near a ravine which would have made impossible the fight between Achilles and Hector as described in the legend. He chose the mound upon which the village of Hissarlik was built, excavated and found the remains of at least nine cities situated one above the other—one of which was the fabled city of Troy.

In 1876 he turned his attention to Greece and the legend of the city of Mycenae as described by Pusanias about 170 A.D. Again his excavations were a success and a great number of golden artifacts, weapons and grave-ornaments were recovered. Although good fortune played its part, his discoveries were successful basically because of his faith in the accuracy of the legends after as much as three thousand years.

Unfortunately, there are very few men with the faith, determination and money of Schliemann today, but there is no shortage of promising legends waiting for the attention of any of his stature who may be interested. There is a Scottish ballad of great antiquity which mentions the castle or "dun" of a clan chief on a headland near Reay in Caithness although there is now nothing to be seen. Perhaps it was just another myth, but in 1751 the Rev. Finlay Cook wrote, "In that year a waterspout fell five miles above Reay and occasioned so great a torrent as to cut a new channel through the sand between Reay and the shore sixteen feet deep, which discovered the remains of a town. The ends of seven houses built in stone were seen in line, and the remains of several others, with some pieces of pavement. The stones, being good quality, were carried off, and the banks soon falling, prevented any further search. Pieces of earthenware were found among the ruins."

This description, not only of the houses but of the means of discovery, is strongly reminiscent of the New Stone-Age village at Skara Brae, north of Stromness on Orkney, which is believed to be at least four thousand years old and was discovered when a storm removed the covering of sand in 1850. A second village was discovered at Rinyo on Rousay island which was partially excavated in 1938. Two hundred and fifty flint implements were found together with pottery which, through the similarity of the markings, suggested a connection with a culture in East Anglia. A third village of this type may throw light upon this minor mystery as well as a check on the accuracy of the ballad. Nevertheless, nobody seems to have given a thought to Cook's report and another village may be there for the digging.

Archaeological investigations, then, sometimes intentionally—sometimes not—are of considerable value in gauging the age and authenticity of folk-legends. There is, in fact, a considerable body of folk-lore in Northern Europe which is connected with the monuments which command considerable attention from archaeologists. So far there has been no serious or concentrated attempt to define or codify the relationships between the two: yet, when we consider the ghosts in gold or silver armour and the burial mound, the connection is perfectly obvious.

It would be necessary to list and codify the legends connected with particular types of monuments and co-relate these with what little we know of the customs and beliefs of our early ancestors, the Celts, the Saxons, the Romans and others, to get a clear idea of the roots from which folk-tales sprang. No definitive attempt will be made at this task in this book, but sufficient attention will be given to this question to throw some light on the origin of the legend of Sawney Bean.

We may wish to question why the stone-age burial mound at Mold was called "The Hill of the Fairies", and why so many mounds, cairns, barrows and the like all over Britain and Ireland are associated with spirits of every kind. In the previous chapter, motif F211.2. indicates how basic this question is, for it is a universal tradition that fairies, elves, spirits, gnomes, goblins, ogres etc, live underground in a great hall the entrance to which is through a mound.

In the best and finest examples of pre-historic mounds, the great hall can actually be found under the mound. In 1968, Dr G. Eogan of the University College of Dublin entered the central chamber of a gigantic mound at Knowth in the Boyne Valley after a number of years of excavation. "I saw a massive chamber (twenty foot high)", he wrote, "I looked up at the corbelled barrel-vaulting and still could not believe how huge it was."[5] If it commanded the respect of Dr Eogan, how fearful and awe-stricken must our primitive forefathers have been—and with what frightful creatures did their imaginations people such structures?

THE MONSTER OF THE MORAR MOUND

"On the shore and forming part of the boundary between north and south Morar, on the west coast of Inverness, is a large, rocky mound, which for many years was very badly haunted. The few people who ventured near it alone after nightfall were invariably found dead and shockingly mangled in the morning.

"Living in south Morar not far from the haunted mound was a man named Macdonail, whose son and heir was a strong, courageous youth of eighteen years of age. One evening Macdonail was visited unexpectedly by a man of considerable importance in the southwest of Scotland. It so happened that just then there was no one in the neighbourhood of south Morar who could help Macdonail entertain so distinguished a guest, so he told his son to go to Bracara and invite certain of his friends there to stay with him for a day or two. He strictly enjoined his son not to return alone at night for fear of the ghost. The young man set out on his mission at once. He passed the haunted mound, which was on the road to Bracara, without molestation and arrived safely at his destination. The people whom he was instructed to invite were unfortunately unable to return with him, and as he could find no one else willing to accompany him, he was obliged to start on his homeward journey alone. Early in the morning his dead body was found close to the haunted mound, horribly mutilated. Around it were traces of a desperate struggle.

"When Macdonail learned about his son's death he swore that he would avenge him. Regardless of the warnings of his friends and relatives, he went alone one night to the haunted mound. He had not been there long before he saw a tall, naked, hairy, headless figure, which came out from behind a rock and said, 'You have come to take your son's ransom. Be wise and go home'. Macdonail in response seized the apparition, and a furious struggle ensued. After it had gone on for a few minutes Macdonail managed to draw his dirk, and he was about to use it when his opponent cried, 'Hold your hand, touch me not with iron, and while there is one within the twentieth degree related to you, I will not be seen again'. Macdonail stayed his hand and found he was grasping air; his sanguinary opponent had suddenly and inexplicably vanished. His account of this extraordinary encounter was widely credited not only in the neighbourhood of its alleged occurence but throughout Ayre."[6]

Beside the usual connection of a spirit or ogre with the mound, there are two other points of interest in this tale—the ogre's fear of iron and the absence of his head. There is a very long tradition that spirits are afraid of iron—"All uncouth, unknown wights are terrified by nothing earthly so much as cold iron."[7] A fifteenth-century tradition assured a mother that her baby was safe from being stolen by fairies if a piece of iron was placed in the cradle and, if you must enter a fairy mound, it has always been considered wise if you thrust a knife into the ground at the doorway so that the door would remain open until you returned. No doubt the superiority of the iron sword over the stone axe or bronze blade introduced this element into traditions connected with the Stone-Age culture whose remains were beneath the mounds and whose spirits roamed abroad.

The matter of heads and headlessness is one on which archaeology has thrown considerable light. In Britain, Galloway, next only to Wales, is steeped in the Celtic tradition, and savants such as Dr Ann Ross have discovered a great deal of information on the religious beliefs of the Celts. Their belief in the magic powers of heads, especially when associated with wells, is well established and to this can be traced the source of a number of traditional tales. In England, one example can be found in George Peele's *Old Wives Tale* (1595) called *The Well of the World's End* in which Zantippa goes with a pitcher to the Well of Life.

She offers to dip her pitcher in when a head rises out of the well and speaks.

Gently dip, but not too deep,
For fear you make the golden beard to weep.
Fair maiden, white and red,
Comb me smooth and stroke my head.

Evidence for the origin of such a tale can be found in the epic stories of the Irish-Celtic Heroes, written down by early Christian monks, which tells of severed heads being washed and combed and offerings placed before them to induce them to utter oracles. This would also be the basis of the famous tales about a head of brass supposed to have been manufactured by Roger Bacon (1214–94) to speak magical secrets.

There are at least seven places called Well of the Heads in Scotland, but Galloway has provided us with several authentic Celtic ritual heads carved from stone; and a traditional tale which must date back at least two thousand years.

THE HEADLESS HORSEMAN OF TYNRON DOON

One beautifully clear night about 1823 Samuel Kirkpatrick, son of the Laird of Cairneycroft, decided to ride over to Penpont to visit his lady. While riding along the road near Clonrae his attention was drawn by the appearance of a large tower with lighted windows upon the top of what was usually a bare hillock on the mountain called Tynron Doon. Something appeared to be descending the steepest side of the hill and was taking a course to intercept him, which it did about half way to Camling where it came onto the road behind him, and as it passed he observed that it was a man on a horse.

The horse was black and wore a saddle-cloth with strange patterns worked upon it and the saddle and bridle was of an unfamiliar design. The man wore armour and great spurs with rowels like saucers—and Samuel saw that he had no head. Realising that this was the famous Headless Horseman of Tynron Doon, Samuel struck spurs to his own steed and gave chase, determined to see where it would all end. Past Penpont he went, past the house of his lady, past Burnhead until they came to the old cross. The sound of singing was heard from within the mound upon which the cross was raised as the phantom came near to kneel in prayer before it.

Samuel dismounted to approach the scene, but as he did so a dog barked at his heels. He turned, but could not see the dog and when he looked again the phantom had also disappeared and the cross stood alone.

This was quite a recent version based upon a much older tradition which told how one of the McMilligans of Dalgarnock went to visit his lady, the daughter of the Great McGachan of Dalquhat, in Tynron Castle. One of her brothers found them together and, not approving of her suitor, struck up a quarrel. Young McMilligan climbed onto his horse and in the heat of temper rode it over the edge of the ramparts at the steepest point so that he and his horse rolled over and over down the cragside. His neck was broken, but more than that, his head became severed and rolled down until it fell into St Bride's Well at the edge of Clonrae. His soul was not permitted to go to heaven without a head and remained earth-bound to ride to the cross on certain nights.

In fact, Tynron Doon is the site of an Iron Age multivallate fort whose periodic habitation up until the seventh century is shown by evidence of excavated items in bone, iron and gold. The story which has been recounted combines the themes of the head-cult of the Celts, the memory of the Iron Age fort transformed into a tower/castle, rowell spurs (which could not have been earlier than the sixteenth century) and the romantic ghost figure of recent times, which shows how it has evolved over the centuries.

Given all these methods of approach it should be possible to throw some light on the origin and evolution of the legend of Sawney Bean. At a first approximation, he appears to be the traditional ogre figure who lived underground emerging only to slaughter and dismember the unwary passer-by. This may be true, but a great number of problems are then presented in accounting for the later additions. Why, for example, should he be presented as living in a cave rather than a mound? (Turning to the original written version of "took up his abode in a rock" offers little help.) And why the elaborate details of his capture and death, when single-handed combat or a cunning trick has sufficed in so many other folk-tales?

In the pages which follow the legend of Sawney Bean will be examined and the following themes given particular attention.

1. The Cave.
2. Cannibalism.
3. The intervention of the king.
4. Death by burning.
5. Missing persons.

Some aspects of the legend, however, must be considered to be embellishments rather than themes. The prolific progeny attributed to Sawney and his wife is *just* possible provided one assumes that they bred like animals and that nature favoured the statistical requirements in selecting the sex of the children. Over the twenty-five years specified, it would be necessary for five of the first six children to be girls and for them to begin to reproduce at the age of thirteen for the figure stated in the legend to be met. In view of the hygiene and rate of deaths in childbirth at the time this is most unlikely.

Even assuming this to be true; at the time of capture the six daughters would have been between the ages of 19 and 24, the eight sons between 11 and 18 and the thirty-two grandchildren between the ages of 3 and 10. The tribe would have been more of a kindergarten than a group of killers; and the women, although being constantly childbearing, would have had to fight like amazons to kill the alleged thousand victims, some of which were on horseback, in twenty-five years.

We must not overlook the fact that such points could have been deliberately introduced to underline the depraved character of the tribe or whoever they were supposed to represent, but there were no fairs of any size in Galloway prior to 1750 and the possibility of a party of twenty or thirty people arriving just in time to rescue the embattled farmer is low in such a sparsely populated area. On the whole, one must regard these embellishments as additions of a comparatively recent date when the requirements for a good story were becoming more sophisticated.

5

In search of the cave

He felt unwholesome dewy cold,
Yet still persued his way—
Resolv'd 'till he had all explor'd,
No more to view the day.
And soon, within a chamber large,
A blazing fire perceiv'd;
And by its flames a sight he saw,
Which else he'd ne'er believ'd.

ANON, *The Legend of Sewen Shields Castle*

There are literally hundreds of caves, or "coves" as they are called locally, on the coast of Galloway and many of them have gathered folk-tales and legends at one time or another. Many are now named after Dirk Haterick and other notable smugglers of the eighteenth century and the original legend has been allowed to die away. None of these caves resemble the description of the cave in the legend of Sawney Bean for various reasons.

A cave having so long a passage would have to be formed in limestone, chalk or similar soft rock and caused by the *outward* flowing of an underground stream. The cliffs of Galloway are of hard Silurian rock—greywacke, shale etc.—which is excavated *inwards* by the sea, especially at an anticline, to form a cave. The waves beating into the cave mouth compress the air within so that it acts as a pneumatic hammer to excavate deeper, but always with a smaller diameter, so that caves along the Galloway coast nearly always take the form of a cone.

This water action tends to play interesting tricks, as we shall see. When a cave is formed on one side of a headland in this way, it will eventually perforate through the base and form an arch which is locally called a Needle's Eye.

That there could not possibly be a cave of the shape and dimensions described in the legend does not, however, mean that there are not any which are, or were, large enough to house his considerable tribe. But this aspect takes on a new significance when it is realised that it is a standard part of Galloway folk-tradition to exaggerate the size and attributes of caves in general. John McTaggart described one cave in the following manner in 1824:

> Pipers Cave O' Cowend. A very celebrated Gallovidian cave in the parish of Colvend; it is situated on a lonely shore, and frequently is heard the sound of bagpipes therein; some think the piper a devil others fancy the musician to be some kind of carline (spirit), who reveres the memory of departed Highlanders, who were anciently smothered in the cave; there is also a bottomless well in it, at least one which lead and chord hath not yet sounded.[8]

Earlier, in 1800, the local minister, the Rev. A. MacCulloch, had also described the cave giving a mixture of tradition and fact.

> Coves or Caves. There are a number of these on the "wild shores of caverned Colvend". The principle of these is called the Piper's Cove, from a legend that a piper undertook to explore it. He carried his pipes with him, and continued to play underground till he reached Barnbarrach, about four miles distant from its mouth. The sound then ceased, and nothing was ever heard again of the unfortunate minstrel. It is found, however, to be only a hundred and twenty yards in length. There is a well in the middle, twenty-two feet deep. Close by the Piper's cove there is a rude natural arch, about forty feet high, called the Needle's Eye.[9]

In this case the description of "caverned Colvend" is very apt. It is a pleasant experience to walk the half mile, at low tide, round the headland from Sandyhills Bay to Portling Bay and observe at least a dozen caves and the Needle's Eye. Unfortunately, the intervening century has taken its toll; the Piper's cave has been pulled down by the sea, the well is filled with sand and there is now no cave in the area greater than fifty feet deep.

S. R. Crockett, faithful to local tradition, continued to magnify caves in his novels—in particular, the small cave on Heston Island (formerly called Rathan) was magnified to the Great Cave of the Isle of Rathan in his romance *The Raiders*.

A further example of the underground piper comes from Dunskey Castle, the ruins of which stands near Portpatrick. The legend tells that Walter de Curry, who occupied it in the fourteenth century, was noted for his piratical raids on the Irish coast. On one occasion he brought back a captive; a piper whom he forced to serve as his minstrel and jester. His jests were not to his master's liking for they smacked of outright criticism and de Curry had him locked in a dungeon to starve to death. The piper found a secret passage which led underground to a cave on the sea shore, but he was unable to escape from this and finally died. Thereafter his ghost was said to be heard playing the pipes and marching up and down on a line where the underground passage was supposed to be.

J. Maxwell Wood wrote that in 1911 there was a cave in the cliff below the castle which was about sixty feet deep, and that when workmen of the Portpatrick water and drainage scheme were digging at the spot in about 1900 they "stumbled upon a large cavernous space at the very place where the reputed sounds of the ghostly pipe music were heard."[10]

Dunskey Castle is quite small and built upon a headland which would have been an ideal site for an Iron-Age peninsular fort. These forts quite often had shallow passages under flat stones where non-combatants—particularly children—were hidden when under attack. If the castle was built upon the remains of a fort, the memory or re-discovery of such a passage, although small, could have prompted this part of the legend.

There is no sign of this cave, or dungeons, today; although there are a number of gigantic crevices around Castle Point which could have been formed by a cave collapsing. The legend is still alive and the piper is still to be heard. The version told to the author in 1973 suggested that the passage led to the District Nurse's House which is near Portpatrick Harbour and almost a mile away from the castle. A walk through the disused railway-cutting (now a footpath) which runs parallel with this imaginary line, with its high walls of solid rock, should disillusion anyone who holds this theory.

There is a simple and logical explanation which may account for the tradition of pipers connected with caves. The pneumatic-hammer effect caused by the sea compressing air in the caves causes the rock to break away in small pieces at weak spots, such as cracks or fissures, and form tiny passages which follow random paths. Until recent years there was a headland on this coast where, when the conditions were favourable, a jet of water, accompanied by hissing sounds, could be seen emerging from a tiny hole on the very top of the cliff and some yards back from the edge. Of course, such a condition is not permanent for more and more rock is broken away, and a larger orifice does not make the same sound. It seems likely that at various caves, over the centuries, wailing sounds not unlike the bagpipes have been made by the sea in this way and inspired a superstitious reaction which gave birth to folk-tales of this sort.

The simplicity of the piper legends indicate that they are very old. When we turn to the 1800s we find the theme has been given a much more sophisticated twist. The following is a tale about Billy Marshall, the leader of the Galloway robbers and gypsies, who died in November 1792 at the age of one hundred and twenty. It is purported to have been told to the writer by Billy's grandson when it was published in *Blackwood's Magazine*.

> Marshall's gang had long held possession of a large cave or cavern in the high grounds of Cairnsmore, in Galloway, where they usually deposited their plunder and sometimes resided secure from the officers of the law, as no one durst venture to molest the tribe in that retired subterraneous situation. It happened that two Highland pipers, strangers to the country, were travelling that way, and falling in by chance with this cave, they entered it to shelter themselves from the weather, and resolved to rest there during the night. They found pretty good quarters, but observed some very suspicious furniture in the cave, which indicated the profession and character of the absent inhabitants. They had not remained long till they were alarmed by the voices of a numerous band advancing to the entrance. The pipers expected nothing but death from the ruthless gipsies. One

> of them, however, being a man of some presence of mind, called to his neighbour instantly to fill his bags (doing the same himself), and to strike up a pibroch with all his might and main.
>
> Both pipes, accordingly, at once commenced a most tremendous onset, the cave with all its echoes pealing back the *Pibroch of Donuil Dhu* or such like. At this very unexpected and terrific reception—the yelling of bagpipes, issuing from the bowels of the earth, just at the moment the gipsies entered the cave—Billy Marshall, with all his band precipitately fled in the greatest consternation, and from that night never again would go near their favourite haunt, believing that the blast they had heard proceeded from the devil or some of his agents. The pipers next morning prosecuted their journey in safety, carrying with them the *spoila opima* of the redoubtable Billy and the Clan Marshall.

Billy Marshall was an historic character in every way worthy of inclusion in such collections of murderers as the *Newgate Calendar* but, somehow, he never made it while Sawney Bean did. The story was clearly inspired by both the Sawney Bean legend and the Underground Piper traditions and is almost certainly the basis of the Dominie's rout of the Bean Clan in Crockett's *The Grey Man.* Presumably the cave referred to is the one overlooking the now disused Cairnsmore station, sometimes called the Door o' Cairnsmoor—which is also mentioned in the *Gallovidian Encyclopedia.*

> Cave o' Caerlauch. Tradition says, that no human eye has ever beheld the back side, or farthest extremity of this cave: that a dog once went into its mouth and came out at the Door o' Cairnsmoor, a place nearly ten miles from it; and when the tyke did come out he was found to be sung (singed), as if he had passed through some fire ordeal or other.

Here, indeed, is a cave of some considerable depth if the tradition be true and well suited to the comfort and character of the Bean Clan; but tradition is not true and we must content ourselves with accepting that only by tradition are all Galloway caves of great length and magnitude and the homes of spirits and ogres which are greatly to be feared.

The superstitious connection between caves and wells is ancient. The supposed magic or healing properties of wells is at least as old as the Celts in Europe, and Galloway has its own equivalent of the famous holy well at Lourdes. At Port Mora, north of Portpatrick, is such a holy well which still exists although unrecognised as such by the passers-by. It was described in the seventeenth century:

> Close by the sea, is a cave, called the Cave of Uchtriemackean, accessible by six steps of a stair, entering to a gate built with stone and lime, at the end of which is a structure lyke ane altar. The people frequent this place the first night of May, and wash diseased children with the water, which runs from a spring over the cave.[11]

A hundred years later (1791) it was still frequented, which was remarked upon with some disapproval by the local minister.

> At the change of the quarter (which is still considered with superstitious reverence) it is usual to bring even from a great distance, infirm persons, and, particularly, ricketty children, whom they often supposed bewitched, to bathe in the stream which pours from a hill, and then dry them in the cave.[12]

Elsewhere the church took positive action as is illustrated by the following extracts from the Dumfries Kirk Session Minutes. "May 2nd 1661: The Congregation is to be advertised that they should forbear going unto Idolatrous wells upon the first Sabbath of May especiallie. James Calland elder is appoynted to take Nottice of such as goe to the Idolatrous well in Troqueir called St. Jorgans well.—May 9th: Elders report that they watched the people last Sabbath as directed."

A still more celebrated cave with a well is St Medan's Cave which is situated on the shore at Kirkmaiden near the tip of the Mull of Galloway and was the home of an early Christian hermit. One might think that the well of the Co' (as it was called), might attribute its healing powers to the sanctity of the hermit, but there is a tradition which indicates that its fame was of greater antiquity.

Less than a mile north of St Medan's Cave is a mound now known as Kirkmaiden Castle but formerly called the Dunnan. It has not been excavated but is probably of pre-historic origin and, in common with many earthworks, it is associated locally with the fairies. As in Ireland, place-names ending in *sheen* (as in

Auchensheen at Colvend) or similar endings indicates that it is a place of the fairies—and there are many such names in Galloway.

An old tale tells of a man sitting on the Dunnan one fine evening when a small woman dressed in green approached him carrying a sick child on her back and a wooden ladle in her hand. She told him she was exhausted and asked him to bring a ladle of water from the Well of the Co' for the sick child. He ungraciously refused, upon which she warned him, using his name although she was a stranger, "never again to sit down on her hoose-riggin (roof) or he might look to it", after which she disappeared. He then realised that he had earned the displeasure of the fairies for the Dunnan was reputed to be their home and he was sitting on the roof. From that day ill-luck dogged all his activities and, the tradition goes, at a later time he again climbed the Dunnan to look out to sea and was stricken with the illness of which he died.

Tradition, then, makes it quite clear that caves in Galloway have just as much significance as burial-mounds or hill forts in many other parts of Europe and wells, whether combined with caves or not, have a similar significance to those in Wales, Northern France and other places which have a strong Celtic background. An ogre could just as properly emanate from a cave in Galloway as it could from a mound in Morar from the folk-tradition point of view. But the folk-tale of the ogre must always originate from an ancient structure which is even older than the tale itself.

If we are to suppose that the Sawney Bean legend is based upon this common stock of folk-tales we must have reasonable evidence to show that the caves were inhabited in pre-history and that they are not merely smugglers' hide-outs which have attracted romantic stories to themselves. Tradition, again from MacTaggart's book, offers a clue.

> Cave o' Cauerlauch. It seems to have been used as a subterranean castle by our forefathers; a clauch or clauchan, or small village, as secure as a caer or castle; so the literal meaning of the whole may be, "the cove of the armed or defended village".

Again the Celtic influence is seen in the use of terms. The famous castle of Caernarvon in North Wales was so named from *caer* and *avon*, or the "castle by the water", by the same Celtic usage of words. If this clue is to be followed we must turn to the science of archaeology for help.

There are many remains of early man in Galloway for it was through this area that the migrating influx of mankind into Scotland began. At a recent count of Iron-Age settlements there were recorded sixty-six hill-forts in Kirkcudbrightshire, sixteen in Wigtownshire and ninety-two in Dumfriesshire; twelve crannogs in Kirkcudbrightshire, thirty in Wigtownshire and five in Dumfriesshire; seven promontory forts in Kirkcudbrightshire and twenty-nine in Wigtownshire. More are constantly being discovered. But before man was able to build in this way—and sometimes after—he lived in caves.

Below the promontory fort situated on Borness Point, on the west of the entrance to Kirkcudbright Bay, there is a cave which has produced plentiful evidence that it was the home of early man.[13] It was described as follows in 1896.

> Borness Point. There are here the remains of an ancient encampment, which must have been a place of great strength and security. The landward side has been protected by a deep double fosse, and nature's own barrier, the steep cliff (they rise upwards of two hundred feet from the sea, in forms irregular, fantastic, and dangerous, while the deep green sea moans along their cavities, or dashes its spray high up their rugged sides), has rendered it secure from the sea.
>
> Close by is an almost inaccessible cave, from the floor of which, in the year 1762, there was dug out great quantities of bones, and traces of human occupation has been discovered. The following, among the remains, were noted by Mr Corris of Senwick, and Mr Bruce-Clarke, who investigated the cave—bones of ox, red deer, goats, horse, pig, pine-marten, rabbit, water vole, and other small rodents, together with numerous remains of birds, and a few frog and fish bones. Intermingled with these occur fragments of bronze, bone needles, and other bone implements.[14]

Torrs Cave, on the east side of the same estuary, yielded a great deal more. The early descriptions of it invited thorough investigation. It was described in the *Statistical Account*:

> From the entrance to the farthest end it measured sixty feet, but the height is unequal. It is narrow at the mouth, then

> gradually widens, rising to a height of twelve feet or more; again it contracts, and through the rest of the sixty feet diminishes. The door had originally been built with stones, and had a lintel, which is now fallen down, and buried under rubbish. The cave itself is a work of nature. From its sequestered situation and difficult access amidst the rocks and precipices, it appears to have been a hiding-place in ancient times. It was not improbably some Druidical Cave.

To this the *Gazetteer of Scotland* added, "The roof is pendant with icicles of stalactite, the constant dropping from which forms on the floor stalagmite crustations. The cave may still be seen, but not the stalactites, by any active person who descends the cliffs."

This cave was excavated between 1934–36 and it was soon found that the "door", "lintel" and "rubbish" were, in fact, the remains of ancient fortifications to protect the entrance to the cave. There had been, over the course of time, no less than eight protective erections in dry-stone which included a stairway, two sentry posts and large stones laid so that entry into the interior was restricted to one person at a time.

Inside the cave itself, "beyond all the structures mentioned, lay charcoal of various occupation-layers, the latest being of Iron-Age date". The Iron-Age levels yielded bones worked for various purposes—scrapers, bones pointed or with holes, a fish hook, pins, Samian-ware pottery; a stone axe, a blue mellon bead, fragments of iron weapons and a bar of bronze. The bones were those of sheep, ox, pig, etc, but "one human bone was found in the packing stones. It was part of a human tibia and had been worked."[15]

There is enough basic material here—Stone-Age occupation, the pile of bones and the hanging stalactites—to suggest the root from which the legend of Sawney Bean may have grown. At first he would have been an ogre without name, but the story would have been elaborated upon in the re-telling. But this is some little way geographically from the traditional cave of the Bean clan, which is under Bennane Head about three miles north of Ballantrae. It was reported, about 1850, to have been some seventy feet deep and wide at the mouth but, again, the sea has reduced it to a large crevice in the rock since then. It cannot be excavated to prove or disprove former habitation, but there are other aspects of this district which throw light upon the problem which have only been revealed in recent years.

Archaeology is a young science which only began to feel its feet in the 1930s. The excavation carried out at Borness Cave in the 1800s was an amateurish activity compared with the painstaking thoroughness with which modern experts would have covered the same ground and produced much more valuable evidence from the same material. This is not intended to belittle the antiquarians in any way, for they did very valuable work, often in the face of ridicule and misunderstanding. An example of this occurred during the excavation of St Medan's Cave. The staunch Presbyterian folk of Portpatrick were so outraged at the salvaging of Catholic effigies and relics from the cave that a mob of them marched a distance of almost twenty miles to wrest the precious "finds" from the excavators and hurl them into the sea from the cliffs of the Mull.

It was not until about 1950 that, due to a series of observations and examinations made by A. D. Lacaille, it was realised that the whole structure of Galloway itself had risen out of the sea by about twenty-five feet since roughly 700 B.C. and that it was necessary to search for original beach-sites at the higher level. As a result of finding early Neolithic stone implements on the west side of the estuary of the River Stinchar, "a shell-mound which stood formerly on the Early Post-Glacial raised beach near Ballantrae harbour", and considering the "relic-yielding terrain between Ballantrae Bridge and Dowan Point", Lacaille concluded that "these flint industries constitute the *earliest unambiguous evidence of man* in the country (Scotland)". The italics are the author's.[16]

Further work was carried out by W. F. Cormack, who found as many as twenty sites of ancient habitation in a year. Most of these were situated where streams had worn a gully down the cliffside, thus supplying fresh water and a means of climbing to and from the shore.

The evidence produced in the next chapter will show that early men were inclined to cannibalism, blood-rituals and similar practices as part of their normal way of life and this is what could be expected of those people who lived at the early sites at Ballantrae and in the Galloway caves. The archaeological evidence for this is supported by the persistent memory which has been woven into folk-lore and expressed itself in the legend of Sawney Bean.

These people did not, of course, live entirely on human flesh as Sawney's family was supposed to do. They lived mainly upon the birds, fish and small animals of the shore which must have been plentiful at the time since the mainland was as deserted as the islands are today. From the mouth of Sawney Bean's cave under Bennane Head can be seen Ailsa Craig, a rocky island about twelve miles away which is still a safe home for sea-birds.

A visitor to Galloway in 1771 mentioned that the Earl of Cassillis rented Ailsa Craig "for £33 per annum to people who come here to take the young gannets for the table; and other birds for the sake of their feathers. . . . The fowler ascends the rocks with great hazard, is provided with a long rod, furnished at the end with a short hair line with a running noose. This he flings round the neck of the bird, hauls it up and repeats it till he takes ten or twelve dozen in an evening." This method of snaring birds is still used on the island of Barra in the Outer Hebrides to this day.

When primitive people did eat human flesh it was either in the face of starvation and death or for ritual purposes in connection with what may loosely be termed their religion. Nor did these practices exist only in the remote past, but continued almost up to the Norman Conquest and played a continuing part in the attitudes of the rest of Britain towards the men of Galloway.

6

Prehistoric Cannibalism

They eat the flesh, and they drank the blood,
And the blood it was so sweet,
Which caused Johny and his bloody hounds
To fall in a deep sleep.

BALLAD FROM THE PERCY PAPERS, 1870, *Johnie Cock*

There is nothing unreasonable in supposing that the people of the Stone-Age—or the later Bronze- and Iron-Ages—practised cannibalism in and about the cave at Ballantrae and the whole of the Galloway area. The weight of archaeological evidence is such that it would be most unusual if they did not, for it was a universal practice.

The story of cannibalism began before the story of true man for the ape-men were cannibals. The Java ape-man was discovered by a Dutch anatomist in 1890, then the Heidelberg Man was found in 1907. Pekin Man was discovered by a British anatomist, Davidson Black, over a period beginning in 1927. All of these were cannibals and lived some five hundred thousand years ago.

Neanderthal Man was the stage just before true man. He lived about 200,000 B.C. in the caves of central Europe, and evidence of his cannibal feasts have been found in the Dordogne (Le Moustier) and at Krapina, Croatia.

Cro-Magnon Man was the first true man and he was also a cannibal if one is to judge from the remains found in the caves of Aurignac near Toulouse. From then onwards, the Stone-,

Bronze- and Iron-Age men left the same sort of evidence. Cannibalism was definitely a way of life to early *homo sapiens*.

The evidence that supports this conclusion is as convincing as it is substantial since it consists of human bones and skulls which have been treated in a way which could only have been done by man (or near-man) and not by an animal. One may readily imagine any large, fierce, hungry animal eating the body of a human being—but one would never find it cracking the bones longitudinally with a stone to extract the sweet marrow. Nor would it slice off a portion of the skull like a breakfast egg to withdraw the brains and, least of all, would one expect it to use a fire to cook these delicacies. There is no gainsaying that this is evidence of man eating man.

Such practices were reflected in the legends of the earliest civilisations. According to the ancient Greeks, when the world began, the god Kronos tried to eat all his own children; Pelops was eaten by Demeter and Atreus served Thyestes' own children to him for dinner. Aristotle in *Nichomachean Ethics*, gives a list of unnatural criminals among which he included "those who provide children for one another to eat".

There is ample evidence of cannibalism in Britain. The Beaker People, invaders from Europe about four thousand years ago, left a refuse pit on the edge of Mildenhall Fell, Cambridgeshire, which suggested a cannibal feast, and when the New Stone-Age part of Maiden Castle was excavated in the 1930s a skull with a cavity was found.

The West Kennet Long Barrow, Wiltshire, contained the "remains of forty-six individuals of all ages and both sexes dating from the Early Neolithic to the Beaker periods—or approximately from the middle of the Third Millenium B.C. to around 1600 B.C.".[17] These bones were studied by Dr L. H. Wells who reported, "A remarkable feature of the collection is that most of the skulls have disappeared, in some cases with their mandibles, but very often without them. . . . It is possible from these (bones) to compose the ghoulish picture of a visitor to the barrow picking up a partly decomposed arm, detaching the humerus, and flinging the other bones into a dark corner."[18]

Recent excavations (1969–73) on an Iron-Age settlement on Danebury Hill, Hampshire, which had been occupied from about 200 to 100 B.C. had evidence which "hinted at grisly rituals using human corpses. Dismembered bodies—arms, legs, torsos mixed with animal bones—were interred in many rubbish dumps."[19]

By this late date man was no longer merely eating his fellow man; he was *doing things* with the dead bodies of his fellow man. From the practical point of view, human bones were worked (as was seen at Torrs Cave) and turned into objects of use or adornment, some examples of these are a knee-cap made into a spindle-whorl, a cup from the crown of a skull and a ladle from an arm-bone.

From another and more important point of view it is clear that the Iron-Age/Celtic people of Europe about the time of the birth of Christ believed that the human body had a magical significance, a belief which they shared in common with all primitive peoples throughout the world. G. Hogg, elaborating on the earlier work of Sir J. G. Frazer, in *Cannibalism and Human Sacrifice*, states it in this way:

> Perhaps the most fundamental, as well as the most universal of these religio-magical beliefs is that a man who eats a part of another man's body will immediately come to possess some of the qualities that belonged to him when he was still alive. . . . For a man to eat the heart of a man he has slain in battle meant he acquired that amount of extra courage; it was all the better if he had been fortunate enough to slay a doughty warrior. The child of an Australian tribesman might be encouraged to eat some part of his father's flesh, so that when he grew up he would resemble his father in his courage, or skill as a tracker, or powers of leadership.[20]

Since practically nothing was written about Scotland *in* Scotland before the Norman Conquest, it is necessary to consider accounts of Celtic practices in Ireland and Europe and conclude that the Celts of Scotland behaved in a similar manner. This is a safe assumption to make for Galloway since it was a cross-roads for the migrations of the Celtic people. If one stands on the Mull on a reasonably clear day one can see Northern Ireland and the Isle of Man. These are ideal conditions for the primitive sailor who depended upon following the coast or line-of-sight navigation. From the Isle of Man can be seen Wales and Southern Ireland and the migration of the Celts from

Northern Europe to the Outer Hebrides, without the aid of navigation instruments, was mainly a matter of persistence and endurance.

They began with a common culture, and a common language. It is well known that the last remnants of the original Celtic language is still spoken in Brittany, Wales and Gaelic (north-west) Scotland; but it is not so widely realised that Welsh-Celtic was the spoken language of Galloway until about 450 A.D. (when early Irish began to appear) and was not completely ousted by Scottish-Gaelic until about 1000 A.D.

From the epic tales of the Ulster Heroes as written down by the early Christian monks, we know that they hung from their belts balls made from a dried mixture of powdered limestone and the pounded-up brains of their enemies. Celtic names for places, sometimes latinised, provide further evidence of the belief in the magical powers of the parts of the human body. *Smetriadum*, in Galloway, has been translated into "the fort of the people who smear themselves with their enemies marrow".

The later invasions of the Norsemen up the whole western coast of Scotland added such rites as blood-brotherhood to this primitive religion, so that when the Norman Conquest provided priestly observers to record what they saw, they also recorded the revulsion they felt.

King Dermot O'Loughlin was an Irish chieftain who spent several years at the Norman court seeking aid to recover his kingdom—and becoming relatively more civilised into the bargain. Aid was eventually given and a Norman force accompanied him to Ireland. After a victory, it is recorded that he had his retainers bring to him the severed heads of the slain, which he examined one by one. He laughed with exultation when he recognised one of them and began to bite at the nose and lips of the dead man.

To him this was the custom of establishing blood-brotherhood with the dead man; a necessary action if he was to prevent the ghost of his enemy from haunting him. To the Christian Normans this was depravity, savagery and blasphemy.

This was the situation about the year 1000 A.D. in all the Celtic lands and from it arose numerous folk-tales—handed from generation to generation by word of mouth—until practically every country in Europe had its folk-tales of cannibalism in one form or another. The eater of human flesh was usually a Giant, an Ogre or, as in the case of Hansel and Gretel, a witch, according to the traditional circumstances or the modifications made in the passing of time. In the case of Galloway, the Ogre seems to have been Sawney Bean—or was later given the name of Sawney Bean, for Bean was probably derived from the Old Scottish word for murderer.

The best example of this form of folk-tale from Britain is called *Childe Rowland*, and a ballad version named *Child Rowland and Burd Ellen* is known, although parts of it are lost. A folk-tale version was known in Aberdeen about 1770,[21] but it was in fact known long before this since Shakespeare included certain lines from it in the ravings of Edgar in *King Lear*, Act III, Sc. iv. which was first produced in 1604.

Child Rowland to the dark tower came,
His word was still,—Fie, foh, and fum,
I smell the blood of a British man.

THE LEGEND OF CHILDE ROWLAND

The King had four children; a daughter, Burd Ellen, and three sons the youngest of which was Childe Rowland. While playing ball together, it was thrown over the roof and Burd Ellen ran to retrieve it but did not return. After a long, vain search the Queen sent the eldest son, acting on the advice of the Wizard Merlin, to seek her in the lair of the King of Elfland. He was instructed that he must cut off the heads of any who spoke to him on the way and while in Elfland must take neither food nor drink.

The eldest son did not return; nor did the second who also went to seek his sister. At last Childe Rowland set out on the quest. Faithfully carrying out his instructions, on the way he cut off the heads of a cow-herd, swine-herd, henwife and ox-herd, all of whom served the King of Elfland, and came at last to the green mound which was its entrance. About the mound he walked three times "widdershins" and cried, "Open door". The mound opened and he entered into a dark cavern dimly lighted by sparkling stones. Within the great hall he found Burd Ellen alive, but under the power of the King of Elfland, and the dead bodies of his two brothers.

Tired by his journey he asked his sister for food and, under the power of the King, she brought it; but before it touched his lips he remembered the wizard's warning and dashed it to the ground. Cunning having failed the King now rushed in, armed and crying—

With fie, and fo and fum!
I smell the blood of a Christian man,
Be he dead, be he living, wi' my brand
I'l dash his harns (brains) frae his harn-pan.

They fought together for some considerable time until Rowland, who was armed with his father's sword, brought the King to his knees pleading for his life, which Rowland promised to spare provided Burd Ellen was released and his brothers restored to life. The Elf-King accordingly produced a phial of red liquid with which he annointed the eyes, lips, nostrils, ears and finger-tips of the brothers and they returned to life. Burd Ellen and her brothers then returned safely home.

This tale has many connections with past beliefs. There is a strong parallel with the Greek legend of Persephone in the return to life from the Underworld and the importance of not taking food during the visit which hints at the very earliest beliefs connected with the sun, nature and the seasons.

The Celtic tradition of the severed head is also included. The early Christian fathers, when seeking converts to Christianity, resorted to a stratagem which had been used by the Romans and others before them. They strove to include suitable aspects of a pagan religion into the Christianity they preached and modified it to suit their own purposes. This they eventually did with the tradition of the severed head; not usually in the mild form we have noted in the *Headless Horseman of Tynron Doon*, but in a way which made the head a symbol of the power of God. Some examples of individuals who attained the status of saints through decapitation are St Winifred of Holywell, in Flintshire, St Lludd of Wales and St Kenelm of Clent.[22]

In Clent, at Cowbach, lieth under a thawn,
His head off-shorn, Kenelm king-born.

The reference to the primitive belief in the magical properties of blood—the phial of red liquid—in Childe Rowland points to a universal belief by primitives of all ages and in all parts of the world. It was long believed, especially when few people died of old age and death usually came in one form of violence or another, that blood was the very essence of life. It seemed logical that if life left the body as the blood also left it, then the return of the blood would also restore life. By the same logic the mingling of blood in a blood-brotherhood ceremony blended together the lives and life-forces of the participants and rendered their fates inseparable.

It is interesting to note that the Elf-King claimed that he was able to *smell* the blood of a man. This attribute has been referred to in many legends from many lands. The German tale, *The Devil with three Golden Hairs*, has a devil which cried, "I smell, I smell man's flesh." The French tale, *Le Petit Poucet*, has an ogre which cries, "I smell fresh flesh." The Norwegian, *Rich Peter the Huckster*, has a dragon which cries, "What a smell there is of Christian bones", and there are many others dating back to the Greek tragedies.

During the hunt for a murder victim in Australia in 1827, a native tracker sniffed out a spot and said, "White man's fat sit down there. Dig here." Three feet below the surface were the remains of Fred Fisher, the murdered man.

One can only assume that pre-historic man was so near to the animal at that stage of his development that he really was able to smell blood just as animals still can, an ability which the most primitive people of our time are just beginning to lose. This being the case, the inclusion of this attribute in traditional tales must be accepted as a matter of course.

The evidence makes it quite clear that man's earliest ancestors were cannibals, but we are not clear whether or not this was a matter of necessity or preference. Montague Summers was of the opinion that man, at that stage, would not necessarily distinguish between the flesh of men and animals.

> Primitive peoples so frequently aligned men and animals in their thinking that it is possible that human flesh was not considered significantly different from other foodstuffs. There is *probably no instinctive aversion* to eating it: the horror shown

> by civilised, and by many primitive, peoples was developed by convention, parallel to their aversion to eating other foods considered unorthodox, unclean, or unfit for human consumption, such as the pig and the dog are unclean for all Semitic peoples. The abhorrence of such foods is an extraordinarily deep emotion, not dictated by biological necessity.[23]

Be that as it may, as time progressed—and certainly during the Iron-Age in Britain—it is obvious that man looked upon human flesh as more than mere food. His growing awareness of, and interest in, the Soul or Life-force of human beings began to form into a primitive religion. He believed that a person had a spirit which, after death, could return and extract vengeance from his killer or ill-wisher and which, for this reason, had to be propitiated. He believed that the life-force could be interchanged between people and this led to ritual cannibalism, human sacrifice, blood-brotherhood rites and similar practices. In 55 B.C. Julius Caesar wrote of the Druids, "They are most anxious to have men believe . . . that souls do not die, but pass after death from one body to another, and regard this as a strong incentive to valour, since the fear of death is lost." He also believed that the various parts of the human body had specific magical properties which he could use if the proper rituals were observed and to this end removed skulls and other bones from the dead.

Later, particularly Christian peoples held such practices in abhorrence to such an extent that they became the characteristics of the arch-villains of subsequent folk-tales. Burial-mounds and similar antiquities were pictured as the entrance to the underworld of evil spirits from which emerged an ogre to attack and feed upon people. With the passing of time, and with the eventual changes of local traditions and conditions, each folk-tale took on a distinctive story although the basis was common to all.

In the case of Galloway it is evident that not only did primitive people live in caves and along the shore, but that there is a body of tradition which associates caves with spirits and ogres and which insists that all caves, no matter what the actual size, shall be considered to have all the space and other attributes required for the Underworld.

The ogres which appeared from the Underworld varied from place to place; the King of Elfland, the Morar Monster, Polyphemus and many others. Sawney Bean conforms to all the requirements of such an ogre, but the later changes and additions are so remarkable as to almost obscure his origins. Just as it was possible, after further examination, to detect a transformation process which changed the traditional tale of Mr Fox to the highly politically-charged story of Bloody Baker, it may be possible to detect the transformation from a basic tale of The Ogre from the Galloway Cave to the Legend of Sawney Bean of the year 1700.

To do this it becomes necessary to discover and examine those local events and historical influences which might have caused the changes.

7

The Wild Men of Galloway

Word is gane to our nobil King,
In Edinburgh, where he lay,
There was an Outlaw in Ettricke Foreste,
Counted him nought, nor a' his countrie gay.

TRADITIONAL BALLAD, *The Song of the Outlaw of Murray*

At the time when the Normans were building their comparatively civilised, comfortable and sanitary castles all over England the natives of Galloway were primitive, savage, warlike and, if not actual cannibals, inclined to use human corpses in horrible ways. They were not particularly backward when compared with the vikings of Harold Hardrada which Harold of England had repulsed, thus allowing William the Conqueror an easier hold on Britain, but as time went on and the civilising influence of Christianity took effect elsewhere the people of Galloway continued in the old ways.

This was partly due to the nature of the people and the isolation of that part of Scotland from the more prosperous and advanced eastern seaboard. While they were nominally vassals of the King of Scotland the local chiefs were, in fact, all-powerful and determined not to amalgamate with the rest of the country. During the tenth century they were noted for slaying priests and monks out of hand and delighted in desecrating Christian churches. They also raided into England to enslave large numbers of young men and women whom they traded to the Irish for cattle.

These independent people looked upon themselves as a separate nation, an idea possibly rooted in the difference of their language. They had a "King" of their own and retained their nordic legal code, the *wergeld*, until about 1426. More importantly, they possessed a very formidable fleet of long-ships which made them a force to be reckoned with. In 1228, according to *The Black King of Man*, an Icelandic Saga, King Alan was said to have lain in wait behind the Mull of Galloway with one hundred and fifty of such ships to attack the fleet of Haco of Norway.

Existing records of this time were written by Christian monks and in them they make obvious their repulsion for the Galwegians. Either the people of Galloway were the most primitive and bestial in Britain or the monks had chosen them as suitable subjects for an anti-paganism propaganda campaign. Whichever was true, the result was to establish a lasting belief in the depravity of the Galwegian.

In the *Saints of Hexham* by Aildred of Rievaulx, the tale of the invasion of England by Malcolm of Scotland, 1079, is told in the following way:

> Malcolm, king of Scots, prepared destruction for the men of Hexham. . . . The king was angry, and summoned his Galwegian vassals, more cruel than the rest, and said in the hearing of the messengers, "So soon as the day dawns, cross the river and fall upon them: let not your eye spare or pitty rank, or sex, or age. Whatever the sword cannot, let fire destroy and leave them no remains."[24]

The invasion of King David of Scotland in 1136 was similarly described:

> David, king of the Scots . . . gathered an army and harried Northumbria with slaughter and fire . . . Hence it was that, when the most cruel nation of Galwegians raged with unheard-of brutality, and spared not sex or age . . . Little children tossed in the air and caught on the points of spears have furnished a delightful spectacle for the Galwegians.

To this description Henry of Huntingdon added further details:

> Now the king of Scots, because he had given an oath to

> King Henry's daughter, acted through his followers execrably, as if under the veil of sanctity. For they cleft open pregnant women, and took out the unborn babe; they tossed children upon their spear-points and beheaded priests upon the altars; they cut off the heads of crucifixes, and placed them upon the trunks of the slain; and placed again the heads of the dead upon the crucifixes. Thus wherever the Scots arrived, all was full of horror and full of savagery. There was the screaming of women, the wailing of old men; groans of the dying, despair of the living.[25]

The Celtic religio-magic symbol of the severed head is seen to be matched against the Christian symbol of the cross in the above, and there is further evidence to suggest that this was more than a battle of armies but was a battle of religions. Richard of Hexham wrote, "It is even reported that in one place they slew many little children gathered together, and draining their blood collected it in a stream which they had previously dammed up and thus drank that bloody water—nay, now for the most part blood."[26]

It would appear that S. R. Crockett was knowledgeable in the early writings about his county for the following extract from Aildred is reflected in his description of Sawney Bean's cave.

> It happened that in the same house were found several little children. A Galwegian stood, and seizing one after the other by both feet struck their heads against the door-post. And when he piled them in a heap he laughed to his comrades and said, "See how many Gauls I alone have slain today". . . . Wearied by the slaughter of innocents, with unwashed knives—with which they had scattered the entrails of their hapless victims—they cut the meats to eat; and mixing with water human blood, they quenched their thirst with the cruel draught, saying they were most blessed whom fortune had preserved to a time when they could drink the blood of Gauls.

These Border skirmishes led to the Battle of the Standard in 1138 which took place on Cowton Moor near Northallerton. The Standard was a ship's mast mounted upon a "machine" or wheeled platform and was hung about with the Host and the banners of St Peter and two local saints. It was sited near to the front of the English ranks so as to inspire the Scots with the fear of the Christian God. The description of the battle, from Aildred's *De Standardo*, gives some idea of the Galwegians as fighting men as distinct from pagan savages.

> King David gathered together his earls and the highest nobles of the realm, and began to discuss with them the array of battle. And it pleased the greater number that the armed men, Knights and archers whom they had should go before the rest of the army, so that armed men should attack armed men, and Knights engage with Knights, and arrows resist arrows. The Galwegians opposed this, saying that it was their right to fill the front line, to make the first attack upon the enemy, to arouse by their courage the rest of the army. The others said that it was dangerous if at the first attack unarmed men met armed men, for if the first rank sustained not the brunt of battle but yielded to flight the courage of even the brave would be readily dispelled.
>
> None the less the Galwegians persisted, demanding that the right be granted to them. "For why art thou so fearful, O King", said they; "And why dost thou so greatly dread those iron tunics which thou seest far off? We surely have iron sides, a breast of bronze, a mind void of fear; and our feet have never known flight, nor our backs a wound . . . we today shall use as shield the valour of our minds, and vanquish these with spears." Then the king . . . yielded to the will of the Galwegians, the two armies then assembled for battle.[27]

The Normans were also discussing their battle tactics, but they took quite a different view of the Galwegian forces. Perhaps with hind-sight, for the Normans won the battle, Aildred put the following words into the mouth of Walter Espec.

> For why should we despair of victory, when victory has been given to our race as if in fee by the most High? Who would not laugh, rather than fear, when to fight against such men runs the worthless Scot with half-bare buttocks? And now they challenge to war their conquerors, their masters; they oppose their naked hide to our lances, our swords and our arrows, using calf-skin for a shield, inspired by irrational contempt of death rather than by strength. Why therefore does the great length of those spears, which we perceive afar off, alarm us? The wood is fragile, the iron is blunted: when it smites it is destroyed, when it is struck it breaks, scarcely sufficing for one blow. Catch it on a stick, and the Scot stands there unarmed. Is it the multitude we fear?

> I say naught of what I think of their number lest I seem to detract anything from your future glory.

Nevertheless, pitted against an enemy armed in a superior manner the Galwegians acquitted themselves well and, although the end could be readily foretold, their enemies were sufficiently just to record their bravery for posterity.

> And the column of Galwegians after their custom gave vent thrice to a yell of horrid sound, and attacked the southerns in such an onslaught that they compelled the first spearmen to forsake their post; but they were driven off again by the strength of the Knights and (the spearmen) recovered their courage and strength against the foe. And when the frailty of the Scottish lances was mocked by the denseness of the iron and wood they drew their swords and attempted to contend at close quarters. But the southern flies swarmed forth from the caves of their quivers, and flew like closest rain; and irksomely attacked the opponents' breasts, faces, and eyes, very greatly impeded their attack. Like a hedgehog with its quills so would you see a Galwegian bristling all round with arrows, and non the less brandishing his sword and in blind madness rushing forward now smite a foe, now lash the air with useless strokes.

These descriptions of the men of Galloway equate them in their beliefs and practices with the Iron-Age Celts of a thousand years before in other parts of Europe. This is why they were called "the Wild Men of Galloway" and "Not men, but brute beasts, devoid of humanity" and we have to accept that they were particularly primitive and backward. Any folk-tale which emanated from this part of Scotland would not evolve or be modified so quickly as it would elsewhere. This may explain why the original basis for the Sawney Bean legend did not turn into a tale of fairies or elves, but retained its primitive aspects unchanged for a longer period and the modifications which did occur were obviously of a later date.

There are two passages in the many writings about the Battle of the Standard which present something of a mystery. The first concerns Chief Thurstan, an ally of the Normans, who had underground chambers dug in the field before the Norman army in which was placed "certain instruments, called in English petronces, which gave forth horrible sounds . . . and when they resounded the wild beasts and other animals which went before the army of the aforesaid King David to assist it, were terrified through fear of the din, and recoiled fiercely upon the army of the same King David."[28]

The second comes from the speech of Espec. The Scots "are preceded by actors, dancers and dancing-girls; we, by the relics of the saints".

No doubt the "instruments which gave forth horrible sounds" were trumpets and these were used by both sides to intimidate the enemy. Giraldus Cambrensis wrote of the Welsh Celts, "In war this nation is very severe in the first attack, terrible by their clamour and looks, filling the air with horrid shouts and the deep-toned clangour of very long trumpets; swift and rapid in their advances and frequent throwing of darts."[29] But what of the reference to the Scottish army being preceded by wild beasts? Could this mean war-dogs or the Galwegians themselves? On the face of it, the reference to actors and dancing-girls is quite absurd unless we take it to be an expression of contempt.

Perhaps the idea was to suggest that the Galwegians were effeminate because they did not adopt the hairsuit-masculine pose of the Normans, for the Celts fought naked. Diodorus Siculus wrote, "Some of them so far despise death that they descend to do battle, unclothed except for a girdle. . . . Some have iron breast-plates of chain-mail while others fight naked, and for them the breast-plates given by nature suffice." Giraldus later confirmed this; "The men shave all their beard except the moustaches. This custom is not recent, but was observed in ancient and remote ages, as we find in the works of Julius Caesar, who says, 'The *Britanni* shave every part of their body except their head and upper lip', and to render themselves more active . . . they are accustomed to cut even the hair from their heads."

Whatever the full implications were, there can be no doubt that until about the year 1200 A.D. these battles were of a religious nature; Christians against pagans, and the weapons used included the full range of propaganda known at that time. Yet the victory was more in the nature of an amalgamation in the long run, for the remnants of Celtic paganism could still be seen in such acts as when the heart of a person was removed, with reverence and in the name of God, and taken to another place to form a shrine.

Nearly forty years after the Battle of the Standard the troubles began again. According to Ralph de Deceto:

> William, king of the Scots, asked again from the king that which in the province of the Northumbrians had been granted, given over and confirmed by charters to his grandfather, king David, and which also had been a long time possessed by him; but meeting with refusal he collected an army, with an endless host of Galwegians—men agile, unclothed, remarkable for much baldness; arming their left sides with knives formidable to any armed man, having a hand most skilful at throwing spears, and at directing them from a distance; raising their long lances as a standard when they advance into battle. Having a safe journey through the lands of Hugh, Bishop of Durham, the king of Scotland began to harry England, to burn down villages, to collect incalculable spoil, to lead away young women captive, to take out the half-living infants from the wombs of the pregnant.[30]

William of Newburgh described it: "By the Scots, to whom no sort of food comes amiss, was gnawed up whatever could be chewed even by dogs. And while they applied themselves to booty, it was the pleasure of this inhuman nation, more savage than wild beasts, to slaughter old men, to butcher children, to disembowel women, and the like; things which it is horrible even to speak of."[31]

The early thirteenth century found things not greatly different under Alan, the last "king" of Galloway. Alan, it must be realised, lived at the time of King John of England and was actually present at the signing of the *Magna Carta* on Runnymede in 1215. He seemed to have been a man of two worlds who was able to cope with the highly civilised existence of the court of England as well as the primitive and savage life led in Galloway. His men were said to have laid waste the land about Carlisle and ravaged Holm Cultram Abbey in exactly the same way as previously described during 1213, an act which in no way squared with the sentiments of the *Carta* which Alan was to support two years later.

At this time there were two brothers, Reginald and Olaf, who contested for the kingdom of the Isle of Man. Reginald had to fly and brought his daughter to Alan for sanctuary. The daughter later married Alan's son and Alan then decided to declare war on Olaf. Alan, his brother Thomas, Earl of Athol, and Reginald invaded Man and laid all the south of the island to waste in 1228, when his men continued to massacre and loot churches as before and, eventually, Olaf was defeated.

Haco, King of Norway, sent a message to Alan demanding that Olaf be restored under threat of war, but Alan replied that it was just as easy for him to invade Norway as it was for Haco to invade Galloway. Haco contented himself with supplying Olaf with men and ships, and this was the fleet which discovered Alan's ships waiting for them at the Mull of Galloway. They hastily withdrew.

Alan died in 1234 leaving three legitimate daughters and one illegitimate son. Since all the daughters were married to Norman barons the independent Galwegians saw that they were in danger of losing all they valued. Their reactions were recorded by Matthew Paris:

> During the same time (1236) many noble and bold men from . . . Galloway, and the island which is called Man, and the regions of Ireland, came together at the insistence of Hugh de Lacy (Lord of Ulster)—whose daughter Alan of Galloway, now deceased, had united to himself in wedlock—on purpose to unite with one accord and to restore Galloway to the baseborn son of Alan aforesaid; crushing with the strong hand the just disposal of the king of Scots. . . .
>
> And that in attempting this they might more surely attain their desire they made an unheard-of covenant, inventing a kind of sorcery in accordance nevertheless with a certain abominable custom of their ancient forefathers. For all these barbarians, and their leaders and magistrates, shed blood from the pectoral vein into a large vessel by blood-letting; and moreover stirred and mixed the blood after it was drawn; and afterwards they offered it, mixed, to one another in turn, and drank it as a sign they were thenceforth bound in a hitherto indissoluble and, as it were, consanguineal covenant, and united in good fortune and ill even to the sacrifice of their lives.[32]

This was the last throw of the dice for an independent Galloway and it lost. The people found themselves under the feudal system of the King of Scotland and although paganism was dying, cruelty and savagery continued. The remainder of Scotland was in an intermediate state; the eastern seaboard was greatly affected by English and European influences and was more advanced, while the northern Highlands were sparsely populated and there are very few records available to enable us to picture life there with accuracy. Galwegians retained their primitive ways longer than any other sections of Britain and the very ferocity upon which they prided themselves caused them to be used as pawns by the kings of Scotland.

They seemed to travel about Britain to a great extent in the roles of mercenaries. They were present in battle at Clitheroe, Lancashire, in 1138, in Yorkshire in 1173, and in the Isle of Man in 1228. They were to fight as far afield as France, but it was during a visit to Moray in 1187 that they met with an incident which may have added another factor to the tradition that was to become the legend of Sawney Bean.

At this time William, King of Scotland, was faced with another contender to the throne named Donald MacWilliam, also known as *Donald Bane*. Since Donald was winning over to his side a number of the king's earls and barons, William decided that the matter of power and kingship had to be settled without delay and set about raising an army.

> King William . . . set out to go into Moray and appointed over his army tribunes and centurions and said to the people: "I also will go forth with you". And the people replied, "Thou shall not go forth, for it is better that you shouldst be a support to us in the city". And the King said to them, "What seemeth to you right, that will I do". And the King remained in the castle which is called Inverness. And he sent his earls and barons with the Scots and Galwegians to subdue his enemy aforesaid. And when they had set out, treason arose among the chiefs; for certain of them loved the King not at all, and certain of them loved him. And the latter wished to proceed, but the others did not permit it. And after dissension they agreed that the chiefs of the army would remain, and should send forward scouts to seize food.
>
> They chose therefore about three thousand warlike youths, whom they sent to seek the King's enemy. And among these was the household of Roland, Utred's son (prince of Galloway); and on the nod hung the decision of all. And when they approached the army of the aforesaid MacWilliam, they made attack upon

> them, and slew MacWilliam himself, and many of his army; and the remainder they compelled to flee and divided their spoils amongst them. And the head of MacWilliam they cut off, and carried it away with them, and presented it to the King of Scotland. And thus, when he was laid low, a great peace arose in Scotland.[33]

Little is known about Donald MacWilliam but we can be sure that he and his followers were just as primitive as the Galwegians. It is important to note that his alias, Donald Bane, meant Donald the Killer—a sort of primitive version of Mac the Knife.

There is no audible difference between the pronunciation of the words *bean* and *bane* in the Galwegian dialect even today, and it seems likely that the spelling of the name in the legend was never formalised until it was written and printed in England in the eighteenth century and then incorrectly.[34]

The present-day dictionary meaning of *bane* is "ruin, destruction, poison or death", which is helpful, but the older words from which it evolved are more specific. The Old Scottish *Bane* and *Baine* meant murder or murderer. The Old English *Bana* and the Old Norse *Bani* both meant death or slayer. This is another example of a "primal root" of a language as described by Baring-Gould. Looked upon in this light Sawney Bean, or Alexander the Killer (since Sawney is Lowland Scots for Alexander, just as Sandy serves further north), is a name not only truly descriptive of his character but rooted in antiquity.

Whether or not the tradition of this name was brought back from Moray by the Galwegians is an open question. It seems more likely they had enough killers of their own and this naming technique (still reflected in the present-day Welsh use of Jones the Grocer etc.) was in use in Galloway too. However, there is a reference in this tale to the king having inaugurated the hunt and, as we have seen, the Galwegians seemed to have used dogs on such occasions, so this particular event may have contributed more than a little to the final form of the legend.

8

James the First *or* Sixth?

Gae prove your speed my billmen bauld,
Yon fellon take or slay,
Alive or dead bring him to me,
Else ye shall rue the day.

SAMUEL WILSON, *Aylmer Gray*

During the period dealt with in the previous chapter the kings of Galloway maintained their independence by playing off the kings of Scotland and England against each other to suit their own ends. In this way they succeeded in holding themselves in a neutral position from which they could take sides with whoever appeared to be winning the seemingly endless war which went on between the two. In a similar manner the local religious houses played the same game for there was a constant, if less bloody, battle between the archbishoprics of Glasgow and York for the Border territory and the souls within it.

After Alan's death there was no question of complete independence. Galloway was ruled by lesser ranks who, nevertheless, continued to play the game as before. A good example of this was the MacDoualls who aided the Scottish army to defeat the Norsemen at Largs in 1263, then, when Edward I of England invaded and camped near Gatehouse-of-Fleet in 1300, sided with him and were rewarded with the marriage of his son to the heiress of Hugo de Champaigne.

It was because of this that when Robert Bruce had managed

to combine the greater portion of Scotland into a nation he found that Galloway still sided with England. He waited until Edward died to invade but had to retreat when an English army lead by the Earl of Richmond approached. A second invasion, led by Robert's brother, Edward, succeeded after two bitter battles. Yet in 1339 Duncan MacDouall decided his position was strong enough to return to the English fold. He swore allegiance and was pardoned for accepting Scots rule. Again the Scottish King invaded and although Edward II sent help in 1342 the game was lost, Galloway remained thereafter a part of Scotland and the MacDoualls rapidly fell from power.

These tactics were a natural outcome of the feudal system under which the King allotted a tract of land to a noble to do with as he pleased, provided taxes were paid and men supplied for battle when called upon. Any noble who could retain the land without paying his dues to his king, by the simple expedient of changing kings whenever necessary, was in a strong position. He also retained complete sovereignty of his lands and people, and became a despot.

The cloak of despotism fitted with ease and comfort upon the leaders of the wild men of Galloway, specially the Douglas clan who ascended as the MacDoualls fell. Their base was Thrieve Castle, now a ruin two miles from the town of Castle Douglas, and they were supported by the smaller land-owners in the district in their constant Border warfare.

Not content with harrying the northern border of England, ten thousand men were taken by the Douglas to fight the English in France in 1423. Arising from this expedition the chief of the clan was able to take to himself the titles of Earl of Douglas, Earl of Wigton, Lord of Galloway, Lord of Bothwell, Lord of Annandale, Lord of Eskdale, Duke of Touraine, Lord of Longueville and Marshal of France.

Their power was so great that the Scottish kings were afraid to interfere with them to any great extent. It is true that during his brief, twelve-year reign (1424–36) James I of Scotland took strong action against the nobles in favour of the Church. In the second year of his reign he called a parliament at Perth where he executed four nobles and took away the land of several others. Two years later he called the Highland chiefs to Inverness, killed three and imprisoned more than forty. But he never did try to interfere with the Douglases. Needless to say, his nobles eventually rebelled and murdered him in 1436.

If, as Nicholson would have had us believe, the capture of the Sawney Bean tribe had taken place during the reign of James I it is unlikely that he would have ventured into Douglas country to hunt the criminals for fear of his own skin. The Douglas clan would have been quite capable of meting out an even more horrible death than burning them without the aid of James or the necessity of conveying them to Edinburgh as we shall soon see.

The death of James left the country under a Regent for his son was too young to rule. By a strange coincidence the sixth Earl of Douglas, who assumed the title in 1440, was a boy of 15 years and the situation bristled with possibilities of plots and counter-plots. Livingstone, the Regent, and Crichton, the Chancellor of Scotland, invited the young earl and his brother, David, to the court to meet the King; Lesley, Bishop of Ross, described the treacherous act that followed. "And after he was sat down to the board with the Governor, Chancellor, and other notable men present, the meat was suddenly removed, and a bull's head presented, which in those days was a sign of execution, (they were given a mock-trial on an unknown charge) the said earl, David, his brother, and Malcolm Fleming of Cummernald, were beheaded before the castle gate at Edinburgh."

The various titles and estates of the Douglases were then divided among other nobles except for Thrieve Castle itself which remained with them. But this madc little difference to the situation for the eighth earl kept a retinue of a thousand armed men at Thrieve and kept the lesser landowners united to him by fear if not by law. The castle had a granite block projecting from the front which was used as a gallows. The earl is said to have boasted that the gallows knob had not been without a tassel for the past fifty years. This was probably no exaggeration for most feudal barons were conferred the right of Pit and Gallows, the former for drowning women and the latter for hanging men—to exercise as they wished in order to maintain peace and order within their own domains. This predilection to punish offenders in a savage way was all very well if it was limited to the sort of miscreants that Sawney Bean was supposed to be, but it was often misused by despots so that they thought it their right to inflict vicious punishments at will.

"Sir Patrick Maclellan, Tutor of Bombie, Sheriff of Kirkcudbright, and Chief of a powerful clan, having taken part with Herries of Terregles, who was his kinsman, against some of the partisans of Douglas, thereby so exciting the indignation of the imperious oppressor that they commenced open hostility against him. He attacked Raeberry Castle, Maclellan chief residence, but finding it impregnable, he succeeded in gaining an entrance by seducing one of the wardens to leave a wicket of the sally-port unbolted on a certain night. By this wicket Douglas entered at the head of a chosen band, and taking Sir Patrick prisoner, carried him off to the dungeon at Thrieve, there to suffer under the power of hereditary jurisdiction. A ladleful of gold was the stipulated reward for the warder's treachery, but when the miscreant appeared at Thrieve to receive the proffered boon, the metal was molten by command of Douglas, and poured down his throat."[35]

The power—and the income—of Douglas was equal to that of the King, and the latter decided to take matters into his own hands. Taking his cue from the example of the "admirable" Crichton in 1440, James II invited the Earl of Douglas to a gathering at Stirling Castle in 1452—with many protestations of friendliness—and killed him with his own hand.

"After supper, at seven o'clock, James of the Fiery Face beckoned Douglas into an inner chamber desiring to confer with him. The interview was a short one, the subject, it is supposed, being the league with Crawford—the King demanding that Douglas should dissolve it. Douglas declared either that he could not or would not do so, which the King rushed on him, exclaiming: 'Then if you will not, this shall!' and struck him with his dagger in the collar and down the body, Sir Patrick Grey finishing the bloody work with a stroke from a pole-axe. Darnley, Boyd, Glendenning, Cranstoun, and Stewart were at hand also, each making officious display of loyalty by stabbing the corpse."[36]

Three years later the King's forces attacked and took Thrieve, the castle became the property of the King and the power of the Black Douglases was broken in Galloway for ever. After that date it was not unusual for the Scottish royalty to visit Galloway—usually on a pilgramage to St Ninian's Shrine—but the possibility of any visit of James I to Galloway is out of the question as is any historical connection with Sawney Bean.

A study of the history of the House of Douglas does more than define their place in the story of Galloway for it provides the first *written* evidence of cannibalism in Scotland. *The Scottish Chronicle* gives a description of the arrival of William Douglas at the siege of Perth in 1341 "bringing with him out of France in five ships, both men of war, and also munitions of armour, artillerie, and weapons, which served the Scotsmen in that season greatly to purpose". Immediately below this description was inserted a paragraph which appears to have no bearing upon the subject matter of the paragraphs before or after it.

> In the same year (as some do write) or (according to others) in the year following, there was such a miserable dearth, both through England and Scotland, that the people were driven to eat the flesh of horses, dogs, cats and such like unused kinds of meats, to sustain their languishing lives withal, yea, insomuch that (as is said) there was a Scottishman, an uplandish fellow, named Tristicloke, spared not to steal children, and to kill women, on whose flesh he fed, as if he had been a wolf.[37]

No mention is made of the location of this incident, but it is assumed that it was in the region of Perth. A similar case was recorded in the year 1460 by Pitscottie. This was the year James II was killed by an exploding cannon and his death was supposed to be preceded by many wonders, one of which was a comet, another the birth of an hermaphrodite who was later burned to death.

> About this time (1460) there was a brigand taken with all his family, who haunted a place in Angus. This mischievous man had an execrable fashion to take all young men and children either he could steal away quietly, or take away without knowledge, and eat them, and, the younger they were, esteemed them the more tender and delicious. For the which cause, and damnable abuse, he with his wife and bairns, were all burned, except one young wench of a year old, who was saved, and brought to Dundee, where she was brought up and fostered, and when she came to a woman's years, she was condemned and burned alive for that crime. It is said, that when she was coming to the place of execution, that there gathered a huge multitude of people, and especially women, cursing her that she was so unhappy to commit so damnable deeds. To whom she retorted with ireful countence, saying, "Whyfore chide you me, as if I had committed

> an unworthy act; give me credence and understand, if you had experience of eating men and women's flesh, you would think it so delicious that you would never forbear it again". So without any sign of repentance this unhappy traitor died in sight of the people.[38]

There is no mention of famine or starvation being the primal cause of their activities in this case and the story might be considered a prototype for the legend of Sawney Bean. There are many similarities, most notable of which is unrepentant death by burning. The writer's use of the term "unhappy traitor" calls attention to other considerations which will be dealt with in a later chapter. Although Angus and Perth were well within the orbit of the King there is no mention of him in either case; and as the chase and capture is not commented upon there are no grounds for comparison.

Neither of these stories have more historical authenticity than the legend of Sawney Bean. All three were written down at a later date as incidents which were *believed to have happened.* No doubt the existence of the headless monster at Morar was implicitly believed by our demon-ridden ancestors and it seems that writers tend to separate folk-tales from supposed historical events according to the credibility of the contents of the tale at the time of writing. The present sharp division between those who find flying saucers credible and those who do not illustrates the point, and it will be interesting to see how the future classifies them.

For the moment it is sufficient to note that the legend of Sawney Bean was not an isolated tale but one of a series of similar tales which extended back into the past, and that in all probability they had a common root. The elimination of James I as a possible actor in all these similar cases now leads us to examine the possibilities for James VI.

In the years between these two monarchs the Galwegians persisted in their warlike ways but, now that they were subservient to the King of Scotland, concentrated their efforts on the Border wars with the English in a manner which eventually aroused the King's displeasure.

These piratical raids were not confined to Galloway but were fought all along the border, but the eighth Earl of Douglas (who was later stabbed by James) took his office of Warden of the Western Border very seriously. In 1448 he summoned a convention at the Convent of Lincluden to revise the laws relating to Border warfare; one of the results of which was:

Intercomming with Englishmen:

> It is founded and ordained by the law of Marches, that no manner of person, man nor woman, of any degree, shall inter-common with any English man or woman either in Scotland or in England, except the prisoners shall come in Scotland, without the special licence of the warden or his deputy asked and obtained in time of warfare, under pain of treason.

Over the years the situation became so bad, and the King so incapable of coping with the unlawful acts of the Border Rievers, that in 1524 James V requested the Archbishop of Glasgow to use the "sword of Holykirk" and curse and excommunicate them. This he did in a long, two-thousand-word statement of great, thoroughness and detail—selections from which are repeated below.

> And therefore my Lord Archbishop of Glasgow has thought expedient to strike them with the terrible sword of Holykirk . . . and proclaim them openly and generally cursed. . . . Therefore, through the authority of Almighty God . . . I denounce, proclaim and declare all such murderers, slaughterers . . . together with their part-takers . . . and defenders of their evil deeds; generally cursed.
>
> I curse their head and all the hairs on their head; I curse their face, their eyes, their mouth, their nose . . . their stomach . . . and every part of their body, from the top of their head to the soles of their feet, before and behind, within and without. . . .
>
> I curse them standing, I curse them sitting, I curse them eating, I curse them drinking. . . . I curse their wives, their children and their servants . . . I wary their cattle, their wool, their sheep, their horses. . . . I wary their halls, their stables, their ploughs, their harrows. . . .
>
> I dissever and part them from the Church of God, and deliver them alive to the devil of hell. . . . I forbid all christians men and women to have any company with them. . . . I declare them partless of all Masses—or other prayers. . . .
>
> And, finally, I condemn them perpetually to the deep pit of hell, to remain with Lucifer and all his fellows, and their bodies

> to the gallows . . . first to be hanged, then riven by dogs, swine and other wild beasts . . . unless they forbear their open sins . . . and make satisfaction and pennance.

Terrible though this curse must have seemed to the average Christian of that century it had very little effect. Things went on as before and any Borderer who really felt in need of the comfort of the Church needed only to cross the border to receive it. It did, however, ensure that the reputation of the Galwegians for being bloody, God-defying men was perpetuated.

The reign of James VI saw very many changes in Scotland as a whole if not particularly in Galloway. The Reformation had changed it from a Catholic to a Protestant country, the power of the nobles was beginning to decline and there had begun an increase in literacy. MacTaggart's comment that "we have volumes, as many as would fill a score of wheelbarrows, all wrote respecting our Kings, Queens and *ither big fowk*, yet hardly a word said about the people", holds true in this case. There is a great deal of written information about James VI in existence, and this is so prolific that if the burning of Sawney Bean and his tribe had occurred during his reign there would be ample evidence available.

As it is, the documents necessary to make the legend "as well attested as any historical fact can be" do not exist. There is abundant evidence to show how deeply James involved himself in the "Fian" plot in 1590, when a number of supposed witches were accused of attempting his life by magic in order to place the Earl of Bothwell on the throne. We know the questions he personally asked the witnesses and the amount of torture applied to the accused; the speeches he made both inside and outside the court and the letters he wrote about it. Similarly we have records of his personal interest and activities connected with the Gunpowder Plot in 1605 and the subsequent torture and trial of Guy Fawkes.

We also know that when a subject interested him deeply he would write a book on the matter, as he did with witchcraft and the dangers of tobacco smoking, and they, because of the importance of the writer, were disseminated far and wide. There can be no doubt that if he had been involved in the case of Sawney Bean in any historical way he would have given the matter the fullest publicity and records would still be available. Furthermore, the religious situation within Scotland at the time was such that there would be other people who would be anxious to seize on the incident to further publicise it for their own ends.

It is also known that James visited Galloway and stayed at his royal castle at Kirkcudbright in 1587. This is well recorded; and if it was thought necessary to record his presentation of a small silver gun to the burgh "to encourage them in the use of firearms" then the Sawney Bean spectacular could hardly have been omitted. The only conclusion to be drawn is that there was no historical confrontation between James and Sawney and, indeed, the possibility of Sawney having existed as a historical person has become very remote, so that we are dealing with a legend rather than a person.

But if there was no reason to include James in the story as a person, there were a number of other reasons for him to be included in the legend, and these will be discussed later since it seems more fitting that this chapter should conclude with an account of the last bloody deeds of the men of Galloway.

Sir Thomas Maclellan, Second Lord of Kirkcudbright and descendant of Sir Patrick already mentioned, became a well-known protagonist in the cause of Presbyterianism during the Reformation. In 1640 he became the colonel of the South Regiment, which was a cavalry regiment chiefly manned by Galwegians. It was part of the army of the Earl of Leven which met and defeated the English at Newburn. In 1644 he attended Parliament and became Steward of Kirkcudbright, succeeding the Earl of Nithsdale. The following year he commanded a regiment of Galwegians, raised at his own expense, which fought with David Leslie at the Battle of Philliphaugh where they defeated the Marquis of Montrose.

The forces of Charles I were being enclosed by a pincer-movement between Cromwell in the south and Leslie advancing from the north. The Marquis of Montrose raised an army in the Highlands and marched south to relieve Charles but Leslie turned north again and they met at Philliphaugh.

The bloody battle that followed is recounted by Patrick Gordon of Ruthven; but it is his description of what happened after the battle, while the remnants of Montrose's army were still fleeing the field, that commands our attention by its familiarity.

> With the whole baggage, which was exceeding rich, there remained now but boys, cooks and a rabble of rascals, and women with their children in their arms, all these without commiseration were cut to pieces; whereof there were three hundred women, that being the natives of Ireland, were the married wives of the Irish; there were many big with child, yet none of them were spared, but all were cut to pieces with such usage and inhuman cruelty as neither Turk nor Scithean was ever heard to have done the like. For they ript up the bellies of women with their swords, till the fruit of their womb, some in the embrion, some perfectly formed, and some ready for birth, fell upon the ground, weltering in the gory blood of their mangled mothers.[39]

Exactly the same charges were being laid against the Galwegians as had been laid five hundred years before. Only fifty years before the legend of Sawney Bean was in print they still had the reputation of being a bloody, merciless band of savages who had fought between themselves and with the English for hundreds of years. Whether or not the reputation was true, either wholly or in part, was beside the point for we are dealing with what people believed and what they handed on to posterity.

9

Horrible crimes that yee are bound in conscience never to forgive

The flame tuik fast upon her cheik
Tuik fast upon her chin;
Tuik fast upon her faire bodye—
She burn'd like hollins green.

TRADITIONAL BALLAD, *Earl Richard*

The reputation for barbarism given to the Galwegians by the Norman priests (as has been indicated in connection with the Battle of the Standard) seems to have been founded on fact, when one considers that these activities continued for centuries. There are however other aspects of such accusations which require further consideration. Accusations of cannibalism have been a popular theme for propaganda since the beginning of recorded history, and it may be that this long-established indoctrination has turned the minds and stomachs of people against eating human flesh rather than the actual taste, digestibility or any other physical aspect of it.

The Romans are known to have accused the Jews and then the Christians of cannibalism. Tacitus used the term *superstitio* in describing the beliefs and practices of the early Christians and it has remained with us as "superstition" ever since. The accusations against the Jews date back to the court of Antiochus Epiphanes of Syria (125–96 B.C.). In his *Against Apion*, Josephus said that Apion's belief that Jews ritually sacrificed and ate a Greek once a year was a typical pagan slander. Roman accusations against the Christians were stronger, and it seems the Christian ceremony of communion misled them to the extent that some believed that they dipped the Host into the blood of a sacrificed child. The slaves of Christians were tortured, according to a letter from the Church of Lyon, to make them accuse their masters of incest and feasting on the bodies of men and children.

For the first four hundred years of the era Christian writers continued to defend the faith from these accusations. Justine Martyr (150 A.D.) said the Jews were responsible for spreading the tales; Titian (170 A.D.), Clement of Alexandria (200 A.D.) and St John Chrysostom (398–404 A.D.) also helped to refute the charges until Christianity grew to a strength which enabled it to accuse the pagans of cannibalism without retort.

By this time Christianity was no longer just another religion among many, it had become so strong—in Europe at least—that it could set about repressing all other forms of religion. The attributes of the pagan gods, and the rituals and beliefs of pagan worship, were branded as demoniacal, anti-Christian and heretic. Canons were constantly issued against worship at pagan shrines (the table of demons) and praying to devils. Pope Hadrian I (772–795) revised and updated a collection of canons attributed to Dionysus Exiguus which were incorporated into the laws of Charlemagne at the council of Aachen in 802.

A few years later the *Corrector* of Burchard, Bishop of Worms, said that women went long distances to kill Christians and eat them or else cut out their hearts and replace them with straw. To the modern reader this is sheer fantasy. The venerable fathers of the Church were either so steeped in hatred for any religion other than their own, or so gullible, that they appeared to believe such accusations without question. They were certainly ready to make authoritative statements and lead the body of Christian worshippers into beliefs of this sort without a shred of evidence.

During the sixth century the Salic Laws imposed a fine of two hundred shillings on a witch who ate a person and the men who carried her cauldron were also fined. One of the laws of Saxony decreed: "If anyone, deceived by the Devil, believes after the manner of the pagans that any man or woman is a witch and eats men, if on this account he burns (the witch) or gives her flesh to be eaten or eats it, he shall be punished by capital sentence", which seems to be aimed at stamping out the belief rather than the offence. Then, in the eighth century, Charlemagne conquered Saxony, forcibly converted the people to Christianity and issued his own laws. One of these decreed, "If anyone sacrifices a human being to the Devil and offers sacrifice to demons as is the custom of the pagans, let him be put to death", and another decrees death for a person who "eats the flesh of witches."

Between the tenth and sixteenth centuries all the accusations made of cannibalism and blood-practices against pagans were progressively made against witches in Europe. Both men and women were supposed to gather at "sabats" or meetings in secret places where they feasted with demons on the bodies of human beings and in the privacy of their own homes were supposed to manufacture potent mixtures from parts of the human body. The records tell of the case of Jubertus (1437) who was supposed to have murdered children and made them into a powder. From the powder imitation children were made for demons to inhabit. So far as the Christian Church was concerned, this was heresy—and the punishment for heresy was burning.[40]

Although literally thousands of people were burned in Europe for being convicted of these crimes the situation in Britain was comparatively mild by comparison, for these beliefs spread slowly and in crossing the Channel they lost much of their potency. The practice of burning witches was never adopted in England although direct dissenters with the established religion were treated as heretics and burned. Witches were burned in Scotland and, again unlike England, torture was used to gain confessions of guilt from them.

Not only was much of the potency of the witch-hysteria in Europe lost in reaching Britain, but it arrived at a later date and the type of heretic-witch who was constantly pursued by the Inquisition in Europe was virtually unknown in Scotland, until a law was passed against them by Mary Queen of Scots in 1563. Mary was the wife of the Dauphin of France and inherited the throne of Scotland on the death of her mother. She brought many European ideas with her and her Act was based on the assumption that witchcraft equated with heresy, hence burning became the prescribed punishment for a traitor, a heretic or a witch—but not for a murderer.

At the same time the Scottish Reformation was taking place. The Protestant John Knox lived to see the Catholic Queen Mary lose her power—she flew to England, Elizabeth I and death—but the punishment of witches remained the same under the reformed church and the persecution of witches was carried out with more thoroughness than before. Although witch-hunting in Scotland continued sporadically between about 1500 and 1700, there were three main peak-periods of activity, 1590–97, 1640–44 and 1660–63.

James the First and Sixth, who plays so important a rôle in the *Legend of Sawney Bean*, was Mary's son. He was born in 1566, crowned the following year when his mother fled, and was brought up from that date under the control of the Presbyterian clergy. As might be expected, he grew up to be a neurotic, if clever, man with a fixation about witchcraft. After his marriage in 1589 his life was threatened by a group of witches motivated by political ends and they were burned to death as both traitors and witches. He became utterly convinced of the reality of witches after this incident and wrote a book on the subject entitled *Demonology* in 1597 which became the text-book for future witch-hunters. According to this he believed that there was a "fearful abounding at this time in this country of these detestable slaves of the Devil, the witches or enchanters". From that time he actively incited the witch-hysteria which created the 1590–97 peak in burnings.

On the death of Elizabeth in 1603 he became the ruler of both Scotland and England, which he ruled jointly until he died in 1625. One of his first acts on coming to the throne of England was to tighten up Elizabeth's Witchcraft Act (also of 1563), although he did not introduce the punishment of burning. In England the punishment was hanging provided that it was proved that the witchcraft caused death, but James changed this to hanging if any form of witchcraft was confessed or proved. It is also very clear that he believed in all the various types of allegations which had been made on the Continent against witches including those of cannibalism and similar rituals, since he introduced the following wording into the Act:

> If any person or persons shall use, practise or exercise any Invocation or Conjouration of any evil or wicked spirit, or shall consult, convenant with, entertain, employ, feed or reward any evil or wicked spirit to or for any intent or purpose; or take any dead man or child out of his or her grave, or the skin, bone or any other part of any dead person, to be employed or used in any manner of Witchcrafts . . . (they) shall suffer the pains of death.

There was probably no other individual who influenced the escalation of witch-hunting in Britain as much as James the First and Sixth and his influence continued long after his death. All the Witchcraft Acts were repealed in 1736 (about the time that the legend of Sawney Bean was circulating in broadsheet form) to the consternation and dismay of many who still believed. A published objection from the Presbytery of the Established Church of Scotland in 1743 said that the repeal was "against the express Law of God".

Naturally, Galloway did not escape this fever. The following story is typical of many.

THE WITCH OF IRONGRAY

"In the reign of James VI of Scotland, or under the early Government of his son Charles, tradition tells of a woman that was burned as a witch in the Parish of Irongray, about seven miles west from Dumfries. In a little mud-walled cottage, in the lower end of the Bishop's Forrest, and nigh the banks of the water of Cluden, resided a poor widow woman, who earned her bread by spinning with a pole, and by weaving stockings from a clue of yarn depending from her bead-strings. She lived alone, and was frequently seen on a summer's eve, sitting upon a jagged rock, which overhung the Routing burn, or gathering sticks, late in a November evening, among the rowan-tree roots, nigh the dells which signalise the sides of that romantic stream. She had also, sometimes, lying in her window a black-letter

Bible, whose boards are covered with the skin of a *fumart*, and which had two grotesque clasps of brass to close it when she chose. Her lips were sometimes seen to be moving when she went to church, and she was observed to predict shower or sunshine at certain periods, which predictions often came to be realised. . . .

"The Bishop of Galloway was repeatedly urged to punish this witch; and lest it should be reported to the King that he refused to punish witches, he at last caused her to be brought before him, nigh to the spot. She was rudely forced from her dwelling, and several neighbours of middle or of old age were dited to declare all the wicked things she had done.

"She was sentenced to be drowned in the Routing burn, but the crowd insisted that she should be shut up in a tar-barrel and hurled into the Cluden. Almost against the Bishop's consent, this latter death was consummated. The wretched woman was enclosed in a barrel, fire was set to it and it was rolled in a blaze, into the waters of the Cluden."[41]

James' beliefs were also those of the Presbyterian church and the General Assembly kept the hysteria inflamed by passing their Condemnatory Acts against witches in 1640, 43, 44, 45 and 49 which caused the second peak in Scottish witch-hunting. The third peak commenced a little early in Galloway, when, in 1659, no less than nine witches were strangled and burned in one day on the banks of the Nith at Dumfries. The sentence was that they "be taen upon Wednesday come eight days to the ordinar place of execution for the burghe of Dumfreis and ther, betuing 2 and 4 hours of the afternoon, to be strangled at staikes till they be dead, and thereafter ther bodyes to be burned to ashes, and all ther movable goods to be esheite".

Witch-hunting began to decline everywhere towards the end of the seventeenth century, but the rate of decline varied from country to country. The last recorded witch-hanging in England was in 1685, but the last recored case of witch-burning in Galloway was in 1698 when Elspeth MacEwen was pronounced guilty of "a compact and correspondence with the devil, and of charms and of accessation to malefices".

THE WITCH OF BOGHA

"Elspeth lived in a solitary house in the farm of Cubbox, called Bogha. As appears from the evidence of two gentlemen who visited her in jail at Kirkcudbright, she was a person of superior education. Still, however, her neighbours were tormented with her, and every calamity that befell themselves or their cattle was attributed to Elspeth's witchcraft. If a cow fell ill, it was Elspeth's doing. It was, also, currently reported and believed that if eggs were wanted (scarce) at New-Galloway, application had only to be made to the old wife of Bogha, and the market was well supplied. But the worst cantrip that she played on the wights of Balmaclellan was the following. She had a pin in her kipple-foot (part of a roof-beam), and when she pleased, could, by taking out that pin, draw milk from her neighbours cows. At length complaint was made to the Sessions, and the Beadle, M'Lambroch, was sent off with the minister's mare to bring her to the Session. Elspeth, after expressing great wonder at this usage from the minister, consented to go. Tradition states that the mare was dreadfully frightened, and, at a rising hill near the manse, since called the 'Bluidy Brae', sweat great drops of blood. After undergoing an examination (with torture), she was sent off to Kirkcudbright, and confined there for about two years. Her imprisonment was rendered so wretched by her tormentors, that the miserable woman implored them to terminate a life so full of suffering. She was condemned, taken to prison, and burned to death in the neighbourhood of Kirkcudbright."[42]

The next two cases in Galloway, in 1703, did not receive the punishment of burning; but in the new and enlightened age of the eighteenth century were banished to Ireland for life. Nevertheless, it was in 1722 that the last witch-burning in Scotland took place. This was in Sutherland, but there may have been later cases in the extreme north where the records are far from complete. It must not be assumed, however, that that was the end of burning people in Britain. Those convicted of Petty Treason—for example, a woman murdering her husband—were punished by burning at the stake until 1790 when the Act was repealed. The cases of Mary Saunders (1746) and Ann Cruttenden (1776) who were burned for Petty Treason both occurred after Johnson's printing of the Sawney Bean legend, so the reader would not find his punishment particularly unusual.

Of the many contributing factors which were formalised into witchcraft beliefs from pagan practices there is one which was particularly strong in northern Europe. It began as a magical ritual where the participants dressed up as animals and, through the action of contagious magic, tried to affect the outcome of the hunt. It had the same purpose as the paintings of animals made by primitive man in deep caves and may well have been practised contemporary with the paintings. Arising from this came stories of beings which were part animal, part spirit and part man which were later to be formalised into vampires, werewolves and the like. Perhaps the best known of these in Britain is Hern the Hunter who is still supposed to haunt the Great Park at Windsor Castle, and whose memory is assured continuance by inclusion in a play of Shakespeare's.

This ritual was known as the wild rout or *wilde jagd* (a term still used for a night of revelry) and the tradition was particularly strong in the area which may now be described as Germanic or Teutonic. Jakob Grimm wrote, "Down to the latest period we perceive that in the whole witch-business a clear connection with the sacrifices and spirit world of the ancient Germans."[43]

The wild rout was a weird group or procession of creatures which banded together on certain nights and, led by a spirit, careered wildly about the countryside devastating and destroying. Any unfortunate person who met them was promptly killed and eaten. Many of the tales about them are evocative of the scene in the legend of Sawney Bean where the wife was pulled down from the horse, disembowelled and fed upon before the eyes of her husband.

The *Sabat* of the formalised witchcraft beliefs was partially based on the wild rout. In this the witches were supposed to gather together and feast on horrible meats, meet and worship their master the Devil and indulge in licentious revelry. After the tenth century most accounts of a *sabat* suggested that they were held in one particular spot and that the aspects of "women travelling long distances to kill Christians and eat them" was practically forgotten. The following traditional tale from Galloway owes more to the wild rout than the *sabat*, and indicates that the cultural heritage of the area contained a great deal that was rooted in the beliefs of their forefathers who had immigated from Scandinavia and northern Germany.

THE GLENLUCE WITCHES

"An ingleside story of the period, handed down as literally true, is that of a labouring man's wife—a sensible, decent woman—having been detained late from home, was returning about the witching hour; and—

> When the grey howlet had three times hoo'ed
> When the grimy cat had three times mewed,
> When the tod had yowled three times in the wood,

—at a spot known as 'Clay Slap' (near Glenluce), she met face to face a troop of females, as to whose leader being cloven-footed she could not be mistaken. Her consternation was the greater as, one by one, she recognised them all, and among them the ladies of the manor. They stopped her, and in her terror she appealed to one of them by name. Enraged at being known, the party declared that she must die. She pleaded for mercy, and they agreed to spare her life on her taking an awful oath that she would never reveal the names of any as long as they lived. Fear prevented her from breaking her pledge, but as one by one the dames paid the debt of nature, she would mysteriously exclaim, 'There's anither o' the gang gone!' She outlived them all and then divulged the secret; adding that on that dreadful night, after getting to her bed, she lay entranced in an agony as if she had been roasting between two fires."[44]

If there was no real historical reason to include James in the Sawney Bean story, there was every reason to include him from the folk-tale point of view for he was the King of the witch-hunters. He did not originate the hysteria, for the belief in witchcraft had been growing until it was necessary for Mary's Witchcraft Act to be passed, but he encouraged it when it might have been discouraged.

If the date attributed to the cannibals of Angus is to be relied upon then the belief was developing a hundred years before James was born, but, when it is remembered that the story was not written down until a few years after Mary's Witchcraft Act, it is impossible to judge how much of the written version was due to current beliefs at the time of writing. It is quite clear, however, that the European line of thought was being followed: cannibals were witches, witches were heretics and burning was the only suitable death for them.

The same reasoning which cast Sir John Baker as the villain of "Bloody Baker", cast James as the hero of "Sawney Bean". They were on opposite sides of the Catholic-Protestant struggle as seen from the Protestant point of view and Catholicism was regarded as heretic and symbolised by witchcraft and cannibalism as a means of engendering religious hatred.

James, who we know wrote to his son that witchcraft practices were "horrible crimes that yee are bound in conscience never to forgive" and wrote in *Demonologie* "In the time of Papistrie, our fathers erring grosslie, and through ignorance, that mist of errors overshadowed the Devil to walk the more familiarlie amongst them", was a "natural" for the role. William Roughead was close to the mark when he saw an affinity between Sawney and James and wrote, "This gentleman was every way worthy to be the subject of so enlightened a monarch", for they were both the originators of senseless death—but perhaps he had overlooked the symbolical implications.

This is probably the most accurate assessment we shall ever get of the current version of the legend at the beginning of the seventeenth century, but it could just as effectively have been set in any part of Scotland. Why was Galloway the chosen scene? This is a question which calls for further investigation.

10

Vampires and Ghouls

> To be knaved out of our graves, to have our skulls taken, are tragic abominations.
>
> SIR THOS. BROWNE

In tracing the connection between Sawney and James two important aspects of the growth of legends and myths have been established. Firstly, that they grew from the abhorrence in which the Christian church held pagan practices which were symbolised by ogres and other evil beings. Secondly, that they tended to continue their existence if they contained, or had introduced into them, aspects which were of topical interest at the time. The second is particularly true of the legend of Sawney Bean when it first appeared in print; for this coincided with a number of historic happenings which were connected in some way either with cannibalism or the misuse of dead bodies.

The hysteria caused by witchcraft beliefs existed on the international level and could hardly fail to be topical; but there were other aspects of folk-beliefs that were contributory factors operating on the national and local levels which will be considered in the next few chapters.

One of the hated proclivities of the pagans was the ritual of blood-drinking. This was introduced into the legend when the Sawney Bean clan attacked the farmer and his wife—"for the female cannibals cut her throat, and fell to sucking her blood with as great a gust, as if it had been wine". This was the aspect of paganism which gave rise to accusations of vampirism by the Church.

The sort of vampires pictured by the Christian fathers had little similarity to Count Dracula and other modern fictitious figures which we now conjure up by the use of the term, although they evolved through exactly the same process as Sawney Bean. The original vampires were usually corpses inhabited by demons which spread evil in the form of the pestilence and plague. The stories about them were of a moral nature showing how God punished the wicked and good triumphed over evil.

The Medieval expert on vampires in Britain was William of Newburgh (1136–1201) who was an Augustinian canon in the priory of Newburgh, Yorkshire. His book, *Historia Rerum Anglicarum*, contains many tales which he had collected from people who really believed that they were true. A typical example of such a tale is—

THE VAMPIRE OF BERWICK-ON-TWEED

"It has come to our knowledge that about the same time a similar and no less great wonder took place in the extreme north of England. There is a fine and flourishing town at the mouth of the river Tweed, called Berwick, which comes under the Jurisdiction of the King of Scotland. Here then dwelt a certain man who was indeed surpassing rich in this worlds goods, but, as later only too clearly came to light, a most infamous villain. Now, after he was buried, at night he used by the power of Satan, as we may very well believe, continually to issue forth from his grave, and to rush up and down the streets of the town, whilst dogs howled and bayed in every direction what time the evil thing was abroad. Any citizen who chanced to meet him was distraught in terror, and then just before daybreak he returned to his grave. When this had been going on for some little time nobody dared step outside his door after nightfall, so terribly did they dread to meet this fatal monster. Accordingly the authorities, as well as men of poor estate, earnestly discussed what steps had best be taken to rid themselves of so sore a visitation, for even the most thoughtless and irresponsible of them were extremely apprehensive lest, if by some unlucky chance they met this living corpse, they would be fearfully assaulted and injured by the dead man; whilst those who were more sagacious and far-sighted were afraid lest, unless some speedy remedy were found, owing to the fact that black decomposition of this foul body horribly infected the air with poisonous pollution as it rushed to and fro, the plague or any other fatal disease might break out and sweep away many, a disaster which had not infrequently been known to happen in circumstances similar to this.

"Accordingly they chose among them ten young men of singular bravery and strength and bade them exhume the accursed corpse. It was then to be hewn member from member and cut into small pieces, and thrown into a blazing furnace so that it might be entirely burned up and consumed. When this had been done the prevailing panic was calmed, 'and the slaughter ceased' (Psalm cv. 30). For the monster, while he was roving abroad by the power of Satan as we have explained, is said to have announced to certain persons whom he encountered that the people should have no rest untill his body was consumed to ashes. Therefore, when he had been burned it seemed in truth as though the people had a certain period of rest, but there very shortly broke out a terrible pestilence which carried off the greater part of the town. And nowhere else did the plague rage so fiercely, although certes, about the same time there was an epidemic in several districts in England."

Sawney's crew were also dismembered as well as burned, so it appears they suffered the fate of vampires as well as that of cannibal-heretics. The origins of many of the aspects of the modern vampire stories can be seen in the above, and the aspect of blood-drinking is not emphasised in that particular example; but when William of Newburgh's only example from Galloway is examined we find it very much in evidence. The incident was supposed to have happened about 1196 and was obtained from a "monk in holy orders".

THE VAMPIRE OF ANNAN

A notorious but un-named criminal fled from Yorkshire to Annan and sought the protection of William de Brus, Lord of

Annandale. (According to the *Lanercost Chronicle*, De Brus had been cursed by Saint Malachy in 1148 for breaking a promise not to hang a man. He seemed to have been a typical "wild man of Galloway"). Under the protection of de Brus, the man continued his wickedness and, although he refused the last rites on his deathbed, was given a Christian burial.

"Going out from his tomb in the night time, by the operation of Satan—a horrible crowd of dogs following, with barking—he used to wander through the streets and around the houses, all persons shutting their doors, nor daring to go out on any business from the fall of darkness to the rising of the sun, lest anyone by chance should meet the monster as he roamed about. But this precaution availed nothing, for the air, being infected by the moving about of his foul body, filled with pestilential exhalation all the houses with disease and death: and now the town, which had been populous a little before, seemed to be almost destitute of life, while those who survived the disaster, lest they themselves, too, should die, moved to other parts. Now, grieving greatly over the desolation of his parish, that man from whom I heard these things desired to summon on the Holy Day, which is called Palm Sunday, wise and religious men who in so great a crisis might give beneficial counsel, and by well-considered consolation might comfort the wretched remnants of the common people. A sermon therefore having been delivered to the people, and the solemnities of the venerable day having been duly fulfilled, he invited to his table his guests, along with the other honourable people who were present.

"As they were dining, two young brothers who had lost their father in that disaster, encouraged each other, said 'That monster destroyed our father, and will soon also destroy us if we take no action. Therefore let us do something manly for the protection of our own health as well as in revenge for our father's death. There is none to hinder while the banquet is being celebrated in the house of the priest, and while all this town is silent as if it were empty. Let us dig up that pestilence, and let us burn it with fire'. Therefore seizing a pretty blunt spade and going to the burial ground, they began to dig. And while they thought that they would require to dig somewhat deeply, suddenly they laid bare the corpse, not much earth having been cast out—the body swollen with enormous corpulence, and the face red and swollen above all measure. But a handkerchief in which it had been wrapped seemed to have been cut entirely to pieces. The young men, whom their anger incited, not being afraid, inflicted a wound on the lifeless body, from which so much blood immediately flowed forth that it might be considered to have been the result of the blood-sucking of many. However, dragging it outside the town, they quickly built a pyre, and, when one of them said that the pestilential body could not burn unless the heart were extracted, another laid open the side with strokes of the blunt spade, and inserting his hand, drew forth the accursed heart, which, having been cut up and the body now burning, it was announced to the dinner party what was being done, and running up they were able to be witnesses of the transaction for the rest of the time. Forthwith that infernal brute, having been so destroyed, the pestilence also, which had been growing worse, was abated among the people, as if by that fire which had consumed the awful corpse, and the air was now purified which had been corrupted by the pestilential motion of it."

There is no other collection of tales about the British vampire like that of William of Newburgh and nothing of any importance followed. These stories seemed to have died out in Britain after the thirteenth century, but not in Europe where the wealth of material was such that the modern vampire story is traditionally set in an East European background.

Released from the original purposes of the priests, the vampire theme passed into the pool of folk-lore and mutated in various ways. The connection between the undead and the plague was soon lost and the necessity for the undead to exist on the blood of the living became a matter of choice. In some cases the undead lost all physical presence and became ghosts and spirits and took unto themselves other attributes, while those which retained it were sometimes activated by other influences than devils.

In the case of Annandale the influence was thought to be fairies. These mischievous creatures who delighted in stealing away human beings, especially by replacing babies with changelings, were also thought to capture and enslave the dead—as is instanced in the following story.

THE UNDEAD SISTER

"One fair Corrie damsel, who was supposed to have died, appeared to her brother, and informed him that she was not dead, but kept in bondage among the fairies, who, after they had carried her off, had left in her bed an image of her, which had been buried in her stead. She entreated him to repair alone to the barn on the following night, set open the doors, and watch there until the hour of midnight, when he would see three forms pass before him, of which she would be the last. She told him he was then to seize fast hold of her, to repeat certain words which she instructed him to use, and that he thus might effect her rescue. Unfortunately, the brother's courage failed him when the hour of trial came, so that the captive sister was never released from elfin thraldom and restored to her family."[45]

Over a hundred years ago and more than ten years before the Folk-lore Society was formed, William Henderson, a student of Scottish folk-lore, had isolated the key to the changing pattern of folk-tales in Scotland.

> On the whole, it certainly appears that the early and medieval churches in their collective form, far from consciously encouraging heathenish superstition, constantly protested against it. Individual clergy in remote districts may have taken a different line, as St Patrick is said to have "engrafted Christianity on Paganism with so much skill, that he won over the people to the Christian religion before they understood the exact difference between the two systems of belief".
>
> At any rate, the old superstition lived on with marvelous vitality, and the Reformation, at least on the Continent and in Scotland, did little to check it. On the contrary, it would seem that when cut away from communion with the angelic world and saints departed, men's minds fastened the more readily upon a supernatural system of another order.[46]

By "a supernatural system of another order" Henderson meant all those beliefs which sprang up under the influence of Presbyterianism as distinct from those associated with the Catholic Church. In the case of witchcraft, as we have seen, there was a complete reversal and where the Catholic Church attributed it to pagans, the Presbyterians, lead by James, attributed it to the Catholics. The rise of Protestantism in England was not proceeding the same way as in Scotland and it is quite possible that if James had not become King of England the witch-persecutions in that country would not have been so severe.

The reasons for this unique situation will be dealt with more fully in the next chapter but, for the moment, it is only necessary to observe that owing to the way in which the evicted Presbyterian clergy stood by their flocks, preaching in the fields at the risk of their lives, many pastors were considered to be semi-divine and many tales are on record of their miraculous acts and of signs sent by God to show his approval of them. This new type of folk-tale was developing at the end of the seventeenth century and the following tale of a vampire, which is certainly expressed in a similar way to those of William of Newburgh, contains more in praise of the pastor than in condemnation of the evil spirit.

THE LEGEND OF ABRAHAM CRIGHTON

'Abraham Crighton, sometime Provost of Sanquhar; though declared a bankrupt before his death (about 1750), the good people of Sanquhar were convinced that he must have somewhere secreted his money, and acted a fraudulent part. On this account it was supposed that he could not rest in his grave, and hence the belief of his frequent appearances in the sombre churchyard, to the affrightment of all and sundry who passed the burying-ground in the evening dusk....

"The exploits of the resuscitated Provost was endless. He assailed all who dared to pass near his resting-place, young and old, men and women. The consternation became universal, the attention of the whole district was directed to the subject, which, indeed, became a topic of discussion throughout the south-west of Scotland....

"At length the matter came to a crisis, and it was found necessary to do something to allay the popular excitement. In those days it was believed that certain sacred charms were effectual in allaying a ghost, and that charm, whatever it might be, was chiefly to be employed by a minister of the gospel. The next thing, then, was to find a person of this order who had the sanctity and fortitude necessary to accomplish the feat. The individual fixed on was a venerable minister of the name of Hunter, in the parish of Penpont (near Tynron-Doon). During the night he went to the churchyard, and on the following day gave out that he had laid Abraham's ghost, and that in the future no person need have the least alarm in passing the churchyard, as he never again would trouble anyone. Mr. Hunter's statement was implicitly believed, and nothing supernatural has since been seen within the ancient burying-ground of Sanquhar.

"To add to the seeming mystery which Mr Hunter wished to keep up, when questioned on what he had said or done to the spirit he replied 'No person shall ever know that'. In order, however, to prevent all such annoyances for the time coming, and to retain Abraham more effectually within the bounds of his narrow cell, it was deemed prudent to keep down the flat gravestone with a strong band of iron or stout chain. This precaution, it was supposed, would keep the popular mind more at ease."[47]

This story was contemporary with that of Sawney Bean; both circulated at the same time and both were topical. The story of Abraham Crighton, however, highlights another historical aspect of the time which would have had bearing on the topicality of both stories. This aspect is connected with the iron band which was placed about the gravestone, and raises suspicions that the iron band was there first and the story offered as an explanation when the real reason for it was forgotten or misunderstood.

There is only one sound reason for graves, at that time, to be protected by iron bands, chains, cages and, in some cases, contain iron coffins with locks—for the protection of the bodies of the dead. Watch-towers were erected in many Scottish cemeteries so that the mourners could watch over the dead with shot-guns to protect them from grave-robbers, or "resurrectionists" as they were sometimes called.

Bodies removed from their graves at dead of night were secretly sold to the Colleges of Surgeons for dissection purposes since there were none to be obtained from official sources. Scotland, having the greater number of Colleges, was the main centre for the "resurrectionist's" trade and hence the main area where fear was felt and precautions considered necessary to ensure the safety of the dead. This was not a sudden occurrence; the College at Aberdeen was founded in 1503, Glasgow in 1637 and Edinburgh in 1721, but grave-robbing activity steadily increased during the late seventeenth century until by 1700 the public were in arms. An outcry was raised in Edinburgh in 1710 and, according to the *Scots Magazine*, there were riots in 1742 which lasted two weeks and the houses of the people accused were burned down.

There were similar riots in Glasgow in 1749, which is just about the time that Provost Crighton died and the prevalent situation may well have prompted his relatives to take precautions against grave-robbers by securing his gravestone with an iron band. If this is true then it appears that the iron band came first and an already existing folk-tale was adapted to explain it.

The trade of the "resurrectionists" lasted for another century. The demand for corpses became so great that they were shipped from the Continent and Ireland concealed in bales and crates and landed at Glasgow, Aberdeen, Leith, Liverpool and London for the clandestine use of surgeons. Such a shipment created a scandal at Glasgow in 1813 and a riot, caused by a mistake, followed in 1822. The Government finally took a hand in the matter and set up the Warburton Select Committee to examine the situation. Even while they were debating, the infamous team of Burke and Hare murdered and sold the bodies for profit to the Edinburgh College.

In 1828, Dr G. S. Pattison, Lecturer in Anatomy at Glasgow University gave evidence to the committee. "In Glasgow, at present," he said, "bodies are so scarce that they are salted in the summer and hung up and dried like Yarmouth herrings." His words are reminiscent of the description of Sawney Bean's cave and we can only conjecture that whispers of such practices had been abroad since the founding of the College at Aberdeen in 1503 adding their quota to the overall pool of folk-tales. However, the Anatomy Act of 1832 ensured future legal supplies of bodies to anatomical schools and the days of the body-snatchers were over.

Returning to the early eighteenth century; too late to influence the printing of the legend of Sawney Bean, but suitably timed to maintain interest, was the historical case of Nichol Brown the

Edinburgh cannibal who was hung in August 1754 for murdering, roasting and eating his wife. His death brought to an end a series of cannibal acts for it was said at the trial that, while drunk, he boasted that he would eat the flesh of Norman Ross, a criminal who had been hanged a week earlier and was still on the gibbet. True to his word, he brought back a piece of leg to cook over the fire of the inn at Leith and ate it in the presence of his drinking companions.

Ironically enough, his own body did not remain on the gibbet for very long for it was secretly taken down at night and thrown into a pond. The authorities retrieved it and again hung it from the gibbet only to find it had again been removed, this time without trace, and, although a reward was offered, it was never recovered. It seems safe to suppose that the body of Nichol Brown ended its career on the slab in the Edinburgh school of anatomy. He may have escaped the flames but not dismemberment.

The early eighteenth century was a period in which there was a tremendous public interest in morbid matters. Public hangings were attended by crowds of people in a festive mood, and prisons and mad-houses were toured by the upper classes as a form of entertainment. Those who were unable to attend such spectacles had to content themselves with written accounts and this brought into being the production of broadsheets and, later, books which filled the need. They were topical, popular and in some way filled a primitive need in human beings which is still being profitably catered for by some sections of the Press today.

The south and south-west of Scotland abounded at that time in incidents which aroused morbid interest yet there were few printers to record them for posterity. The legend of Sawney Bean was admirable for this purpose but it was the English printers who put it on record and not the Scots. Perhaps the printers at Edinburgh had little interest in stories of Galloway; or perhaps the English printers had other reasons which prompted them.

11

The Savouriest Pie of a Child Chaldron

> Dayly experience makes it appear;
> For instance, lately on the Borders,
> Where there was nought but theft and murders,
> Rapine, cheating, and resetting,
> Sleight of hand in fortunes getting.
>
> WM. CLELAND, 1697, *Poems*

The year 1066 was probably the most important date in British history. The advent of the Norman Conquest brought about changes which have affected people to this day. Not the least of these changes was the introduction of Christianity on the continental pattern and the anti-pagan beliefs that went with it. Such churchmen as Aildred of Rievaulx, who were steeped in these beliefs, were the only persons capable of recording history as they saw it. The result was inevitable; the records were biased and the Galwegians acquired a reputation which was not to be envied. By contrast, readers of the works of Giraldus Cambrensis (1147–1223) will note no similar bias against his fellow Welshmen (although they were Celts contemporary to the Galwegians) because he did not possess the continental attitudes towards the paganism about him.

The situation in Galloway is illustrated by a minor mystery of the district. Dundrennan Abbey, which was founded in 1142 and colonised by monks of the Cistercian Order from Rievaulx in Yorkshire, has been long known for the great number of monuments it contains. One of these depicts a prior standing upon a human figure which is naked save for a kilt. The heart of the prior is pierced by a dagger yet he remains upright upon the prostrate body.

The original purpose of this monument is not now known, but it is assumed to be a symbolical representation of a priest who had been murdered by a wild man of Galloway but who, nevertheless, triumphed through the victory of the Christian Church. Nowhere else is a monument of this sort to be found; perhaps there was no other place where it was thought to be suitable or necessary.

The bloodshed which went on in Galloway for the next three hundred years was not wholly a religious matter, however, for the Galwegians were also involved in what might be called a political struggle. They had no wish to submit to Norman feudalism—although they had to submit to a Scottish, clan-oriented version of it in the end.

In the whole of Britain, between the fifteenth and eighteenth centuries, the relationship between religious and political rivalries was so complex and interconnected that it was sometimes quite impossible to separate them. As we have seen in the case of James I of England, the Protestants came to look upon Catholics as cannibal-witches who were only fit to be destroyed, and as time went on these accusations were made against political opponents quite separately from any religious implications. In short, accusations of cannibalism were an early form of political propaganda.

During the Great Rebellion in England, when Cavalier fought Roundhead in a contest which was as much a religious as a political war, the Cavaliers stood for the King and the established Church while the Roundheads supported a republic and a Puritanical faith. One Roundhead might fight because he opposed the King's taxes while his companion was prompted by religious motives only. In such circumstances the accusations were used freely for either reason. According to Sir Walter Scott:

> The terror preceding the civil wars, which agitated the public mind, rendered the grossest and most exaggerated falsehoods current among the people. When Charles I appointed Sir Thomas

Lunsford to the situation of Lord Lieutenant of the Tower, the celebrated John Lillburn takes to himself the credit of exciting public hatred against this officer and Lord Digby, as pitiless bravoes of the most bloody-minded description, from whom the people were to expect nothing but bloodshed and massacre. Of Sir Thomas Lunsford, in particular, it was reported that his favourite food was the flesh of children, and he was painted (a portrait) in the act of cutting a child into steaks and broiling them. The colonel fell at the siege of Bristol in 1643, but the same calumny persued his remains, and the credulous multitude were told,

The post who came from Coventry,
Riding in a red rocket,
Did tidings tell how Lunsford fell,
A child's hand in his pocket.

Many allusions to this report, as well as to the credulity of those who believed it, may be found in the satires and lampoons of the time, although, says Dr Grey, Lunsford was a man of great sobriety, industry and courage. Butler says, that preachers

Made children with their lives to run for't,
As bad as Bloodybones or Lunsford.[48]

Lunsford died two years before the Battle of Philliphaugh and the dreadful massacre that followed, and we may have doubts as to just how much of Patrick Gordon's account is truth and how much propaganda, for it is quite clear that such accusations were being used freely at that time. The reputation that the Galwegians already had would be enough to ensure that the accusations would be believed.

In order to illustrate that this type of propaganda had by no means fallen into disuse at the time of the printing of the legend of Sawney Bean, it will be useful to consider that other terror, the French Revolution.

The main driving force behind that uprising against the Catholic Church and the King of France were the *Sans Culottes* or Middle Class—craftsmen and shopkeepers—and, although they had no actual political power, their influence forced many political issues. It was they who stormed the Bastille in 1789, mobbed the Tuilleries in 1792 and surrounded and attacked the

Convention in 1793. They were loyal to France and the Republic (which made them the natural enemies of the British and the Government of William Pitt), and the source of French policies which affected Britain.

Again the old accusation of cannibalism was produced and was typified by a cartoon executed by James Gilroy, an Englishman, which depicted a typical *Sans Culotte* family seated at table and eating the corpses of their victims in a manner strongly reminiscent of the Bean clan. The stored and hanging portions of human bodies about the room, the child being roasted over the fire and an eye-ball being eaten with gruesome relish were details included with the intention of arousing hatred against the revolutionaries.

Perhaps Gilroy had knowledge of the historical case of Gilles Gamier (1574) who made a practise of attacking girls before he killed them and ate their flesh. He sometimes took home a joint for his wife. This, and similar actual incidents of cannibalism which happened from time to time, probably added just that touch of authenticity which made the basest of propaganda acceptable to the credulous.

Almost immediately after the close of the Great Rebellion in England there arose another religio-political situation in Scotland, which did not affect England, but affected Galloway to a considerable extent and gave birth to a new type of folk-tale in the area. Following the intentions of Charles I; Charles II, followed by his brother, James II, attempted to force Episcopy upon the Scottish nation. The determination of the people to resist the appointment of Bishops over them was regarded as a form of revolution and was ruthlessly put down. "The whole face of the government looked more like the proceedings of an inquisition, than the legal courts; and yet Sharp was never satisfied".[49]

The people fled from the churches and held services in the fields but a law of 1670 made this punishable by death and those who were captured were butchered on the spot. In desperation, the people retaliated and Archbishop Sharp of St Andrews was pulled from his coach on Magus Moor in 1679 and murdered—and the persecution of Covenanters was redoubled.

> The short reign of James II was ushered in by an act of singular barbarity. A few weeks after this bad man came to the throne, all the children in Annandale and Nithsdale, between the

> ages of six and ten, were seized by soldiers, separated from their parents, and threatened with immediate death. The next step was to banish, by wholesale, large numbers, of adults, who were shipped off to unhealthy settlements; many of the men first losing their ears, and the women being branded, some on the hands, some on the cheeks.[50]

James II, who reigned from 1685–88, had a sadistic nature and seemed to enjoy the sight of torture, for the following was writen about him during his visit to Scotland.

> When any are to be struck in the boots, it is done in the presence of the council; and upon that occasion, almost all offer to run away. The sight is so dreadful, that without an order restraining such a number to stay, the board would be forsaken. But while he (James) had been in Scotland, was far from withdrawing, that he looked on all the while with unmoved indifference, and with an attention, as if he had been to look on some curious experiment.[51]

Many of the officers who were appointed by the kings acted in a very similar manner and to them Galloway in particular was a hot-bed of insurrection. There were particular circumstances in Galloway which made it a very strong Presbyterian area. The famous John Welsh, an early Protestant minister, married Elizabeth Knox, daughter of John Knox, when he was the minister of Kirkcudbright, and, after he had moved to Ayr in 1599, was banished to France for his zealous preachings. His grandson (also John Welsh) was the minister at Irongray until he was ejected in 1662, after which he preached in the hills and fields at the risk of his life and took part in the so called Pentland Rising. With the example of many ministers of this type to follow the people of Galloway upheld the principles of the Covenant and were persecuted as a result.

The stories of the cruelties perpetrated by the King's men in Galloway are seemingly endless. The worst of them was probably that of two women who were tied to stakes in the sea where they were left until the incoming tide drowned them. These may be read elsewhere, but below are three examples of funeral monuments which, with many others, can still be seen about the area. Most of these stones were erected and carved long after the event by the famous "Old Mortality" (Robert Patterson) who made it his life's work "to keep in rememberance the righteous". Sir Walter Scott met him in 1793 and subsequently wrote a novel which immortalised him.

At the Parish church at Dalry:

> MEMENTO MORI
> Here lyrth Robert Stewart (son of Major Stewart of Ardoch) and John Grierson, who were murdered by Graham of Claverhouse, Anno 1684, for their adherence to Scotland's Reformation and Covenants, National and Solemn League.
>
> Behold! a stone's here forced to cry,
> Come see two martyrs, under me that ly.
> At Water of Dee, they ta'en were by the hands
> Of cruel Claverhouse, and's bloody bands.

In Kells churchyard:

> MEMENTO MORI
> Here lies Adam M'Whan, who, being sick of fever, was taken out of his bed and carried to Newton of New-Galloway; and next day most cruelly and unjustly shot to death by the command of Lieutenant-General James Douglas, brother of the Duke of Queensberry; for his adherence to Scotland's Reformation Covenants, National and Solemn League. 1685

On a stone a quarter mile away from Irongray church:

> Here lies Edward Gordon and Alexander M'Cubbine, martyrs, hanged without a law by Lagg and Captain Bruce, for adhering to the Word of God, Christ's kingly government in his own house, and the covenanted work of reformation against tyranny, perjury and prelacy.
> Rev. xii. 11.
>
> As Lagg and bloodie Bruce Command,
> We were hung up by hellish hand;
> And thus their furious rage to stay,
> We died near kirk of Irongray.
> Here now in peace sweet rest we take,
> Once murdered for religion's sake.

These memorials denounce the two great perpetrators of atrocities in Galloway—the Duke of Queensberry and the laird of Lag. The entire affair was of a highly emotional nature and I quote the present Curator of the Burgh Museum, Dumfries, as stating that within the last thirty years "middle-aged people" were seen "going through the motions of spitting on the floor, in sheer hatred, at the sight" of a chair in the Museum which had once been the property of the Laird of Lag. As a result of this hatred which had been felt over a period of three hundred years these two men have been regarded as ogres and woven into the fabric of the folk-tales of Galloway.

THE LEGEND OF THE DUKE OF QUEENSBERRY

"Concerning the death of the Duke of Drumlanrig, *alias* Queensberry (who was appointed High Commissioner to James II in 1684), we have the following relation: That a young man perfectly well aquainted with the Duke (probably one of those he had formerly banished), being now a sailor and in foreign countries, while his ship was upon the coast of Naples and Sicily, near one of the burning mountains, one day they espied a coach and six, all in black, going towards the mountain with great velocity; when it came past them they were so near that they could perceive the dimensions and features of one that sat in it.

"The young man said to the rest—if I could believe my own eyes, or if I ever saw one like another, I would say that is the Duke'. In an instant they heard an audible voice echo from the mount—'Open to the Duke of Drumlanrig!' Upon which the coach, now near the mount, vanished. The young man took pen and paper, and upon his return found it exactly answer the day and hour the Duke died."[52]

There were numerous tales connected with Robert Grierson of Lag Tower also known as the Laird of Lag, Bloody Lag, Bloody Grier and Auld Lag. Perhaps the most famous of these is Wandering Willie's Tale in Sir Walter Scott's *Redgauntlet*, where he was seen to be supping in hell with Claverhouse (Queensberry), but an authentic Galloway tradition is repeated here.

THE LEGEND OF BLOODY LAG

"The year of grace, 1733, was wearing fast towards Yule, when one stormy night a small vessel found herself overtaken, at the mouth of the Solway, by a gale wind that was almost too much for her. Close-hauled and fighting for every foot of sea-way she was slowly forcing her way up-channel against the angry north-west blast when a strange adventure befell her. In a lull following a savage squall the moon broke through the black flying clouds, lighting up the storm-tossed sea and revealing to those aboard another struggling sail far astern.

"Curiously, the seamen gazed, but searching glance gave way to wonder, and wonder to fear, when they saw what at first seemed a craft like themselves, come rushing onwards in the very teeth of the wind, and with as much ease as if running 'free' before it. The moon dipped, and again darkess descended on the face of the waters, but not for long. Once again the moon-light pierced the curtain of flying cloud. Then was seen what surely was the strangest craft that ever sailed the tossing Solway sea—a great State-coach, drawn by six jet-black horses, with out-riders, coachmen, and a great retinue of torch-bearers, footmen, and followers, furiously driving onwards over the foam-crested waves. As the phantom carriage plunged nearer, the skipper, regaining some little of his courage, ran forwards, hailing in sailor fashion—'Where bound and where from?'—and the answer came back, clear and distinct across the raging waters—'To tryst with Lag! Dumfries! From—Hell'."[53]

The association of the principal characters in these two tales with Hell and the Devil indicates their place in the evolution of folk-tales. The anti-paganist policies of the Christian Church, begun in the eleventh century, evolved into accusations of witch-craft; and witches, together with other miscreants, were later considered minions of THE DEVIL, a single symbolical personi-fication of all possible evils. Even if we had no other way to date the lives of Lag and Claverhouse, it would be possible to date the stories about them with reasonable accuracy; and by the same principle the original legend of Sawney Bean must be older than the middle of the seventeenth century. A later version, perhaps the printed version, might have had a political significance.

The situation throughout Britain became such that in 1668 James II began to fear for his life and fled to the Continent with his family. The execution of Charles I had forever removed any possibility of later monarchs regaining their divine rights; James went too far and courted a similar death. Once in exile, however, he and his descendants made repeated efforts to regain the throne and another period of political terror began for Britain. The Stuart invasions of 1715 and 1745 commenced in the Highlands of Scotland and the armies marched south in the general direction of London. On the latter occasion they traversed practically half the length of England before they turned back at Swarkestone, near Derby, when the help they expected did not arrive.

The men who fought in these invasions were Highlanders who had no real loyalty to the Stuart cause, but were mainly interested in the loot to be gained. This was the main reason for the failure of the rebellions, for once the Highlanders had gained sufficient loot to satisfy themselves they were in the habit of slipping back home, leaving their leaders to carry on the fight as best they might.

> The Highlanders obtained a glorious booty in arms and clothes, besides self-moving watches, and other products of civilisation, which surprised and puzzled them. Excited by such acquisitions, a considerable number could not resist the old practice of their people to return to their glens, and decorate their huts with their spoil.[54]

For all this, while the Highlanders were actually under arms they were completely merciless, savage and bestial and there seemed to be no limit to the lengths to which they would go. It is reported that during the 1715 rebellion they committed "horrible outrages on corpses which they had dug up"; and during the 1745 rebellion it was reported that "the late Mr Halkston of Rathillet, who had been in this expedition, told Mr Young that the belief was general among the people of England, that the Highlanders ate children."[55]

These accusations were propaganda in all probability, but it must be realised that the people of England were in a state of fear because of the unexpectedness of the attack, particularly when the Union of Scotland and England in 1707 seemed to offer a promise of peaceful co-existence. Furthermore, from the English point of view, the invaders were seen to enter the country from the region of Galloway and march south by way of Carlisle. If the legend of Sawney Bean had been in print since 1700 (and it was certainly in print before the 1745 rebellion) it may well have been a contributing factor to the view which the English took of their attackers.

The city of Carlisle had a special relationship to Galloway due to its proximity on the other side of the Border and was continually subjected to attacks from the Scottish side over the centuries as has already been indicated. During the Great Rebellion Carlisle was a Royalist stronghold and was fair game for the Scottish Protestant forces which were marching south to the aid of Cromwell, and the English Protestant (and anti-royalist) forces. David Leslie, with four thousand horse and foot (whose activities after the Battle of Philliphaugh we have already noted), captured Newcastle-upon-Tyne in 1644 and then crossed the country to give siege to Carlisle in October of that year. It held out until June 1645, but when Charles I lost the Battle of Naseby they realised there was no hope of relief. The townspeople submitted to the Scots who remained there until December 1646 when the alliance between the Scottish and English Protestants was dissolved. Two years later the town was re-taken for Charles but, in the end, surrendered to Cromwell.

Carlisle fared a little better in 1715 because the invaders surged about the town and passed on south without attacking it. The surrounding countryside, however, suffered. In 1745 the town was besieged again and the semi-civilian Militia Regiment, which garrisoned it, mutinied and fled at the sight of the Scots. Again aid was not forthcoming. General Wade, the road-builder, was garrisoned with his troops at Newcastle, but, as he had not then built a road between Newcastle and Carlisle, he was unable to bring up troops in time and Prince Charles Edward entered Carlisle on November 18th, triumphantly riding upon a white horse and preceded by a hundred pipers. The town remained in Scottish hands until the rebellion was put down and Parliament hurriedly pushed forward the work of building a road between Newcastle and Carlisle. In engineering this General Wade astutely used the substantial foundations of Hadrian's Wall, so that the greater part of it was lost to posterity.

If there was any town which had justification for hurling abuse at the Scots, and the Galwegians in particular, it was Carlisle and it seems quite reasonable to suppose that the enterprising printer who first published a broadsheet version of the legend of Sawney Bean was Jollie and Sons of Carlisle. If so, it was probably based upon a folk-tale which had been known in the locality for many years. It is even probable that the mothers of the Carlisle area had hushed their children with the threat "Sawney the killer will come and get you".

There were printers established in Newcastle, the only other Border Town of importance, from 1646, but they did not publish the legend so far as can be ascertained; Sawney Bean, however, would not have been of local interest to them.

The next chapter recounts *The Murder Hole*, a Galloway folk-tale, which presents yet another aspect of the legend of Sawney Bean.

12

The Murder Hole

With breath drawn in, the murderous crew
Stood listening to the yell;
And greater still their wonder grew,
As on their ear it fell.
They listened for a human shriek
Amid the jarring sound;
They only heard, in echo's weak,
The murmurs of the hound.

JOHN LEYDON, NORTHUMBRIAN BALLAD, *The Court of Keeldar*

THE MURDER HOLE (A Galloway Tale)

In a remote district of country belonging to Lord Cassillis, between Ayrshire and Galloway about three hundred years ago, a moor of apparently boundless extent stretched several miles along the road, and wearied the eye of the traveller by the sameness and desolation of its appearance; not a tree varied the prospect; not a shrub enlivened the eye by its freshness, nor a native flower bloomed to adorn this ungenial soil. One "lonesome desert" reached the horizon on every side, with nothing to mark that any mortal had ever visited the scene before, except a few rude huts that were scattered near its centre; and a road or rather pathway, for those whom business or necessity obliged to pass in that direction.

At length, deserted as this wild region had always been, it became still more gloomy. Strange rumours arose that the path of unwary travellers had been beset on this "blasted heath", and that treachery and murder had intercepted the solitary as he traversed its dreary extent. When several persons, who were known to have passed that way, mysteriously disappeared, the enquiries of their relatives led to a strict and anxious investigation; but, though the officers of justice were sent to scour the country and examine the inhabitants, not a trace could be obtained of the persons in question nor of any place of concealment which could be a refuge for the lawless or desperate to horde in. Yet, as inquiry became stricter, and the disappearance of individuals more frequent, the simple inhabitants of the neighbouring hamlet were agitated by the most fearful apprehensions. Some declared that the death-like stillness of the night was often interrupted by sudden and preternatural cries of more than mortal anguish, which seemed to arise in the distance; and a shepherd, one evening, who had lost his way on the moor, declared he had approached three mysterious figures who seemed struggling against each other with supernatural energy, till at length one of them, with a frightful scream, suddenly sunk into the earth.

Gradually the inhabitants deserted their dwellings on the heath and settled in distant quarters, till at length but one of the cottages continued to be inhabited by an old woman and her two sons, who loudly lamented that poverty chained them to this solitary spot. Travellers who frequented this road now generally did so in groups, to protect each other; and if night overtook them they generally stopped at the humble cottage of the old woman and her sons, where cleanliness compensated for the want of luxury, and where over a blazing fire of peat, the bolder spirits smiled at the imaginary terrors of the road, and the timid trembled as they listened to the tales of terror and affright with which their hosts entertained them.

One gloomy and tempestuous night in November, a pedlar boy hastily traversed the moor. Terrified to find himself involved in darkness amidst its boundless wastes, a thousand frightful traditions connected with this dreary scene darted across his mind; every blast, as it swept in hollow gusts over the heath, seemed to teem with the sighs of departed spirits, and the birds, as they winged their way above his head, appeared, with loud and shrill cries, to warn him of approaching danger. The whistle with which he usually beguiled his weary pilgrimage, died away in silence, and he groped with trembling and uncertain steps, which sounded too loudly in his ears. The promise of Scripture occurred to his memory, and he revived his courage. "I will be unto thee a rock in the desert, and as a hiding place in the storm." Surely thought he, though alone, I am not forsaken, and a prayer for assistance hovered on his lips.

A light now glimmered in the distance which would lead him, he conjectured, to the cottage of the old woman; towards that he eagerly went his way, remembering, as he hastened along, that when he had visited it the year before, it was in company with a large party of travellers, who had beguiled the evening with these tales of mystery which had so lately filled his brain with images of terror. He recollected, too, how anxiously the old woman and her sons had endeavoured to detain him when the other travellers were departing; and now, therefore, he confidently anticipated a cordial and cheerful reception. His first call for admission obtained no visible marks of attention, but instantly the greater noise and confusion prevailed within the cottage. They think it one of the supernatural visitants of whom the old lady talks so much, thought the boy, approaching the window, where the light within shewed him all the inhabitants at their several occupations. The old woman was hastily scrubbing the stone floor and strewing it thickly over with sand, while the two sons seemed with equal haste to be thrusting something large and heavy into an immense chest, which they carefully locked. The boy, in a frolicsome mood, thoughtlessly tapped at the window, and they all instantly started up with consternation so strongly depicted on their countenances, that he shrunk back involuntary with an undefined feeling of apprehension. Before he had time to reflect a moment longer one of the men suddenly darted out of the door and, seizing the boy roughly by the shoulder, dragged him violently into the cottage. "I am not what you take me for," said the boy, attempting to laugh. "But only the poor pedlar who visited you last year."

"Are you alone?" enquired the old woman in a harsh deep tone, which made his heart thrill with apprehension.

"Yes," said the boy, "I am alone here, and alas!" he added, with a burst of uncontrollable feeling, "I am alone in the wide world also! Not a person exists who would assist me in distress, or shed a tear if I died this very night."

"Then you are welcome!" said one of the men with a sneer, while he cast a glance of peculiar expression at the other inhabitants of the cottage.

It was with a shiver of apprehension, rather than cold, that the boy drew towards the fire, and the looks which the old woman and her sons exchanged, made him wish that he had preferred the shelter of any one of the roofless cottages which were scattered near, rather than trust himself among people of such dubious aspect. Dreadful surmises flitted across his brain, and terrors which he could neither combat nor examine imperceptibly stole into his mind, but alone, and beyond the reach of assistance, he resolved to smother his suspicions, or at least not increase the danger by revealing them. The room to which he retired for the night had a confused and desolate aspect; the curtains seemed to have been violently torn down from the bed, and still hung in tatters around it; the table seemed to have been broken by some violent concussion, and the fragments of various pieces of furniture lay scattered upon the floor. The boy begged that a light might burn in his apartment till he was asleep, and anxiously examined the fastening of the door, but they seemed to have been wrenched asunder on some former occasion, and were still left in that condition.

It was long ere the pedlar attempted to compose his agitated nerves to rest, but at length his senses began to steep themselves in forgetfulness, though his imagination remained perfectly active, and presented new scenes of terror to his mind, with all the vividness of reality. He fancied himself again wandering on the heath, which appeared to be peopled with spectres, who all beckoned him not to enter the cottage, and as he approached it vanished with a hollow and despairing cry. The scene then changed, and he found himself again seated by the fire, where the countenances of the men scowled upon him with the most terrifying malignity, and he thought the old woman suddenly seized him by the arms, and pinioned them to his side. Suddenly the boy was startled from these agitated slumbers by what sounded to him like a cry of distress; he was broad awake in a moment and sat up in bed, but the noise was not repeated, he endeavoured to persuade himself it had only been a continuation of the fearful images which had disturbed his rest, until on glancing at the door, he observed underneath it a broad red stream of blood silently stealing its course along the floor. Frantic with alarm, it was but the work of a moment to spring from the bed, and rush to the door, through a chink of which, his eye nearly dimmed with affright, he could watch unsuspected, whatever might be done in the adjoining room.

His fear vanished instantly when he perceived that it was only a goat that they had been slaughtering, and he was about to steal into his bed again ashamed of his groundless apprehensions, when his ear was arrested by a conversation which transfixed him aghast with terror to the spot.

"This is an easier job than you had yesterday," said the man who held the goat. "I wish all the throats we've cut were as easily and quietly done. Did you ever hear such a noise as the old gentleman made last night? It was well we had no neighbours within a dozen miles, or they must have heard his cries for help and mercy."

"Don't speak of it," replied the other, "I was never fond of bloodshed."

"Ha! Ha!" said the first with a sneer, "you say so, do you?"

"I do," answered the other gloomily, "the Murder Hole is the thing for me that tells no tales, a single scuffle, a single plunge and the fellow is dead and buried to your hand in a moment. I would defy all the officers in Christendom to discover any mischief there."

"Ay, Nature did us a good turn when she contrived such place as that. Who that saw a hole in the heath, filled with clear water, and so small that the long grass meets over the top of it, would suppose that the depth is unfathomable, and that it conceals more than forty people who have met their deaths there? It sucks them in like a leech!"

"How do you mean to dispatch the lad in the next room?" asked the old woman in an undertone. The elder son made her a sign to be silent, and pointed towards the door where their trembling auditor was concealed; while the other, with an expression of brutal ferocity, passed the bloody knife across his throat.

The pedlar boy possessed a bold and daring spirit, which was now roused to desperation, but in any open resistance the odds were so completely against him, that flight seemed his best resource. He gently stole to the window; having by one desperate effort broken the rusty bolt by which the casement had been fastened, he let himself down without noise or difficulty. "This betokens good", thought he, pausing an instant in dreadful hesitation as to what direction to take. This momentary deliberation was fearfully interrupted by the hoarse voice of the man calling aloud, "The boy has fled, let loose the bloodhound!" These words sunk like a death knell in his heart, for escape now appeared impossible, and his nerves seemed to melt away like wax in a furnace. "Shall I perish without a struggle?" thought he, rousing himself to exertion, and, helpless and terrified as a hare pursued by its ruthless hunters, he fled across the heath. Soon the baying of the bloodhound broke the stillness of the night, and the voice of its masters sounded through the moor, as they endeavoured to accelerate its speed. Panting and breathless the boy pursued his hopeless career, but every moment his pursuers seemed to gain upon his failing steps. The hound was unimpeded by the darkness, which was to him so impenetrable, and its noise rung louder and deeper in his ear, while the lanterns which were carried by the man gleamed near and distinct upon his vision.

At his fullest speed, the terrified boy fell with violence over a heap of stones, and having nothing on but his shirt, he was severely cut in every limb. With one wild cry to heaven for assistance, he continued prostrate on the earth, bleeding, and nearly insensible. The hoarse voices of the men, and the still louder baying of the dog, were now so near that instant distruction seemed inevitable; already he felt himself in their fangs, and the bloody knife of the assassin appeared to gleam before his eyes—despair renewed his energy, and once more, in an agony of affright that seemed verging towards madness, he rushed forward so rapidly that terror seemed to have given wings to his feet. A loud cry near the spot he had left arose on his ears without suspending his flight. The hound had stopped at the place where the pedlar's wounds had bled so profusely, and deeming the chase now over, it lay down there, and could not be induced to proceed. In vain did the men beat it with frantic violence, and tried again to put the hound on the scent, but the sight of blood had satisfied the animal that its work was done, and with dogged resolution it resisted every inducement to pursue the same scent a second time. The pedlar boy in the meantime paused not in his flight till morning dawned and still he fled, the noise of steps seemed to pursue him, and the cry of his assassins still sounded in the distance. Ten miles off he reached a village, and spread instant alarm through the neighbourhood. The inhabitants were aroused with one accord into a tumult of indignation; several of them had lost sons, brothers, or friends on the heath, and all united in proceeding instantly to seize the old woman and her sons, whose names were Mackillop, and who were nearly torn to pieces by their violence. Three gibbets were immediately raised on the moor, and the wretched culprits confessed before their execution to the destruction of nearly fifty victims in the Murder Hole which they pointed out, and near which they suffered the penalty of their crimes. The bones of several murdered persons were with difficulty brought up from the abyss into which they had been thrust, among whom was the father of the pedlar boy, the old gentleman before mentioned who had just returned from abroad. So narrow is the aperture, however, and so extraordinary the depth, that all who see it are inclined to coincide in the tradition of the country people that it is unfathomable.

The scene of these events still continues nearly as it was three hundred years ago. The remains of the old woman's cottage, with its blackened walls (haunted of course, by a thousand evil spirits), and the extensive moor, on which a more modern inn (if it can be dignified with such an epithet) resembles its predecessor in everything but the character of its inhabitants. The landlord is deformed, but posesesss extraordinary genius; he had himself manufactured a violin, on which he plays with untaught skill, and if any discord be heard in the house, or any murder committed in it, this is his only instrument. His daughter has inherited her father's talent, and learned all his tales of terror and superstition, which she relates with infinite spirit. When she describes with all the animation of an eyewitness, the struggle of the victims grasping the grass as a last hope of preservation, and trying to drag in their assassin, as an expiring effort of vengeance, when you are told that for three hundred years the clear waters in this diamond of the desert have remained untasted by mortal lips, and that the solitary traveller is still pursued at night by the howling of the bloodhound, it is then only that it is possible fully to appreciate the terrors of the MURDER HOLE.

13

Missing Persons

It was a mirk mirk night, and there was nae stern light,
And they waded through red blude to the knee;
For a' the blude, that's shed on earth,
Rins through the springs o' that countrie.

TRADITIONAL BORDER BALLAD, *Thomas the Rhymer*

The Murder Hole, reproduced in the previous chapter, is from *Historical and Traditional Tales*. Nicholson probably collected this from the February 1829 issue of *Blackwood's Magazine*. Although based upon an ancient tradition, it shows evidence, particularly in the final part, of being re-written during the early nineteenth century. The fullness of the descriptions, the use of conversation and the final reference to the present inn-keeper to "round off" the story indicates the sophistication of the writer.

The unknown author was modest in the changes he made to the original folk-tale when putting it in a form which would please the readers of his time. By contrast, Sir Walter Scott, for example, moved the life of "Old Mortality" back one hundred years in time to produce the effect he wished to make, and the embellishments that Prest and Crockett made to the legend of Sawney Bean have already been described. The result is that it is not too difficult to detect the basic motif in the *Murder Hole* as being the need to account for missing persons and the memory of human sacrifices.

There are numerous stories of "murder inns" from all over

Europe, and those readers who have seen that uproarious Fernandel film *The Red Inn* will appreciate just how flexible the theme can be. It will be remembered that it was first assumed that the victims of Sawney Bean had fallen into the hands of such people and that some inn-keepers were executed on suspicion only, which prompted others to change their occupations. Probably some murdering inn-keepers really did exist, but it would not have been essential for them to live in lonely places and prey upon lonely travellers to ply their trade.

A brief examination of the geography of Galloway makes it clear that the areas which have always tended to be reasonably habitable are the low-lying areas along the sea-coast and the river valleys leading inland. All the north and east of Galloway consists of uninviting upland separated by valleys. At one time these uplands were thickly wooded and were the home of wolves, bears and wild boar—to quote only those animals which were a danger to human life. This made travelling hazardous enough without the additional dangers of the wild men of Galloway. Nevertheless, people did travel and many never arrived at their destinations. Consequently those real or imaginary murderers of travellers would be presumed to carry out their horrible trade on lonely stretches of road which were used by travellers with reasonable frequency.

In early times the coast road was the only one of any significance in Galloway, and travellers from Ireland, or the South, who were moving north through Galloway, chose this road in preference to the difficult passes over the Glenkens. These travellers, if the legend is to be credited, had to pass through the area in which Sawney Bean and his clan operated, which may account for the high number of victims attributed to him. The keepers of the inn in *The Murder Hole*, however, had much less opportunity than Sawney Bean to prey upon travellers simply because fewer of them passed their way. The legend of Sawney Bean thus has yet another root in the practices of the Iron-Age people of Galloway, but this is better traced through the implications of the story of *The Murder Hole*.

There were two well-known murder holes in Galloway at the time that Nicholson re-printed the stories, which leads to some confusion as the tale is far from specific about its location. Tradition and Sir Herbert Maxwell locates one of them at

Rowantree near the foot of Loch Doon—which accords well with the "murdering inn-keeper" theme, since it is near a mountain pass now traversed by the A713 road from New Galloway to Ayr. It has been described as follows:

> There was a natural pit of unknown depth, with a narrow mouth, peering into which one might see—nay, see to this day, inky water lipping to the green moss growing around the orifice. This murder hole has never revealed the full tale of its secrets, for it cannot be cleared out; but it was to its depths that the remains of the victims were one by one committed.[56]

The hole has since been filled up, "to prevent it being a danger to children and sheep", says the Rev. C. H. Dick in the 1938 edition of his book, "but the site can be seen in a hollow of the moor just below the sheep-rees of Craigenreoch".

The other murder hole was at Loch Neldrican, a spot on the Rhinns of Kells where very few travellers would have passed, and was described by M. M. Harper as follows:

> A part of this most eastermost end of the Loch, level as a green where they play bowls, and in daylight the same smooth colour, but in the midst a black round eye of water, oily and murkey, as though it were without a bottom, and the water a little arched in the middle. A most unwholesome place to look upon.[57]

A more scientific description would be that there was a geological fault (perhaps a glacial sink-hole) beneath the shallow waters of the loch, greatly increasing its depth over a small area and preventing the shallow-water plants from growing. The result was that an almost perfect circle of clear water appeared among the plants. This was clearly illustrated in Dick's book, but the caption named it as the Loch Doon murder hole, although the text was not in error. The 1938 edition corrected this mistake and informed the reader that it was then smaller and had lost its circular shape.

Perhaps S. R. Crockett had inspired this mistake for he had described the disposal of victims here in his novel *The Raiders*. May Maxwell pointed it out to the hero, Patrick Heron, while still holding the bloodstained knife with which she had stabbed to death a bloodhound which had been pursuing him in the manner of the pedlar boy in *The Murder Hole*.

Nicholson added a footnote to the story. "An account of this Murder Hole was communicated by Mr Train to Mr George Chalmers author of *Caledonia*, and is thus referred to in that work vol iii, page 234: 'This Murder Hole is said to be eighty feet deep from which human bones have been brought forth'. The origin of these Murder Holes 'have been referred to the feudal grant which conferred the right of Pit and Gallows on so many Barons, the former for the drowning of women, the latter for the hanging of men'." This might have been a reasonable theory to put forward at the time, but the discoveries of archaeologists since that date have made it clear that finding bones in this way does not necessarily imply that the person was the victim of that sort of killing (particularly now that the carbon-dating process can date the age of the bones with reasonable accuracy).

It has to be accepted, and evidence was given in an earlier chapter, that Iron-Age man in Britain, as well as many other countries, venerated and made offerings to the gods or spirits of wells, streams and lakes by throwing into them whatever it was thought would please the spirit. The donor really did make a personal sacrifice by giving to the god a possession which he or she prized highly.

There is a lake called Dow-Dhu (Black Loch) near Penpont and Tynron Doon which retained its reputation for healing powers until the nineteenth century, when parcels of food were sometimes found floating on the water as offerings to the spirit of the lake. The *Statistical Account* gives some idea of the ritual involved when a person went to the lake on behalf of a sick friend.

> He had to carry a part of the dress of the person ailing, or the furniture of the animal bewitched, as an offering to the spirit of the loch. . . . But when the person had reached it, he had to draw water in a vessel, which was on no account to touch the ground—to turn himself round with the sun—and to throw his offering to the spirit over his left shoulder—formalities all indicative of druidical origin—and to carry the water, without having once looked back, to the sick person or animal, to be drunk. All this, moreover, was to be done in silence.

People, perhaps captured enemies, would be cast into the water in ancient times as tokens of thanks to the spirit for the successful outcome of a battle. Objects of precious metal which have been preserved to this day by the mud which received them, were, until recently, the main evidence of such sacrifices. There is a lake near Toulouse which the Celts held sacred and into which they threw many offerings of metal. According to the records, when the Romans overran the district they sold this lake, and others, by public auction to the highest bidder because of the amount of precious metal it contained.

This method of sacrifice was no less prevalent in Galloway than in any other Celtic land and many examples of metal objects have been found which support this contention. Probably the most spectacular of these was a great bronze cauldron filled with one hundred and ten items of Iron-Age workmanship which was found in Carlingwark Loch by fishermen in 1862. The items included chain mail, a gridiron, and weapons and implements of all kinds. A plough-beam was found in a bog near Lockerbie in 1872, and the metal portions of a pony-cap and a drinking horn were recovered from Torrs Loch (near Castle Douglas) which was dated to about 300 B.C.

Several other finds—the Birrens Horsetrappings, the Plunton Armlet, the Middlebie Horsetrappings, the Lochar Collar, the Balmaclellen Hoard and others—are dated to about the second century A.D., because of the similarity of the decorations on them with a famous hoard found at La Tene in France, and this provides another link with the cultures, practices and beliefs of the peoples of Europe at that time.

Human remains or any organic material do not usually last for more than fifty years or so in the ground unless the chemical conditions are favourable. For instance peat bogs (which are not present in Galloway), are often conducive to the preservation of organic materials and are responsible for the finds of "Bog Butter" in Ireland. These are small wooden tubs of butter which were thrown into the bog as an offering to the spirit of the place during the Iron-Age and which have been well preserved to this day.

Under such circumstances it would seem that objective, archaeological evidence to show that human beings were sacrificed by being thrown into water would be impossible to obtain except by a stroke of incredible luck. Fortune smiled on the archaeologists in 1954 when men digging in the Tollund peat bog in Denmark uncovered a body at a depth of eight feet, which had been preserved by the chemicals in the peat. Paul Johnstone, who assisted Dr Glyn Daniel to make a film report for the B.B.C., described it thus:

> The man was naked except for a leather belt and cap, and the cause of his death was clearly visible, a leather noose drawn tightly round his neck. Thanks to the tannic acid in the peat, which had stopped the normal decaying action of the bacteria, his body was extremely well preserved, and it was at once taken with great care to the National Museum at Copenhagen for further study.
>
> The dating was helped by the fact that a number of other bodies, none of them intact, have been found in northern Europe in similar circumstances. This, together with the depth of the peat, seemed to indicate that the body dated from the Iron-Age and was about two thousand years old.[58]

In this case he may well have been a willing sacrifical victim for his features are serene (the head is still preserved) and he had eaten a cooked meal a little more than twelve hours before his death. Perhaps he believed that he was giving his life for the benefit of his tribe. In any case the ritual which accompanied his death differed from those which required that the skull be removed, and included strangling before his body was thrown into the water—just as a witch was strangled before being thrown into the flames.

There are many circumstances which indicate that sacrifices of human beings, and later animals, were made in Scotland and elsewhere especially when the spirit of the dead was expected to guard the place or building from evil spirits. There is a tradition that St Columba called for a volunteer from his followers to give his life in this way when the Abbey was erected on Iona, and as late as 1703 the practice was echoed in the case of the man who was brought before the Kirk Sessions at Oyne, Aberdeenshire and accused of burying a cat under the hearth of his new house.

The story of the *Murder Hole* appears to be a latter-day retelling of a folk-tale which originated from knowledge of ancient Celtic practices, but the basis of this and many other tales is the wish to account for missing persons by minds which were superstitious and dark with fear. Unless the bodies of the missing persons were found, perhaps attacked by men or wolves, they were deemed to be the victims of some night-monster which spirited them away to an evil death.

Sawney Bean was the greatest of Scotland's night-monsters. His field of activity was the most fruitful in Galloway, the main coast-road, and his victims numbered far more than any others. The bodies were not merely thrown into a pool, or dismembered as were the victims of the Morar Monster, but used as a grisly witch-feast. The heads were removed and the severed limbs scattered and sometimes thrown into the sea to be cast up at distant places.

There was no indignity that had ever been known which Sawney Bean did not inflict upon the corpses of his victims. In any other place in Europe he would have been the Devil, but the Christian concept of the Devil came late to Galloway and Sawney remained supreme as the figure in which was contained all the evils of paganism.

14

Some Conclusions

Here where once Druid's trod, in times of yore
And stain'd their altars with a victim's gore
Here, now, the Christian ransomed from above
Adores a God of mercy and of love.

From a plaque near the entrance of the Banwell Bone Cave in the Mendip Hills.

In the preceding chapters we have reviewed all the events and influences which may have contributed to the existence of the *Legend of Sawney Bean* as we know it today. The traditions and folk-tales which have been mentioned are but a selection from a greater body which have been handed down from past generations and were recorded in print. For each one so preserved there must have existed many more which have now been forgotten. The information is necessarily incomplete, but it is suggested that there is enough to trace the history of the legend.

There can be no doubt in the face of the archaeological evidence that cannibalism has been practised since the human race began. We have no idea why this was so, but since the beginning of recorded history two or more thousand years ago man has eaten man either because he was desperately hungry, for magical purposes or because the insanity of occasional individuals tended that way, and we have no reason to suppose that there could be any other reason in earlier times.

Although direct evidence is lacking at this time it cannot be presumed that the people of the Mesolithic culture who lived at Ballantrae, Loch Ryan, Low Clone, Barsalloch and other prehistoric sites in Galloway were different in this respect and it would be unreasonable to do so. Whether or not one accepts that the practice of cannibalism already existed in Galloway before the Iron-Age, or whether one prefers to believe that the Iron-Age invaders brought such customs with them, there can be no doubt whatever that such rituals were performed throughout Britain as well as in Galloway before the arrival of the Romans.

Of the Iron-Age, Celtic peoples there is a great deal of concrete evidence to be considered. Their dwellings, burial places and shrines have been excavated throughout Britain and Europe, and the Galloway remains at Torrs Cave, Tynroon Doon and other locations show that the area was not exceptional in any way. They all made a common practice of doing unwholesome things with the corpses of human beings.

It was not until after the arrival of the Romans, followed by the advent of Christianity, that records were made in Latin which illustrate these heathen practices in a way that archaeology cannot do, and out of this emerged our understanding of the basic pattern of beliefs at that time. Magical powers, operating through spirits, were attributed to caves, streams and wells, the human head and human blood. There was a belief in a human spirit which had an after-life in the underworld and probably other aspects of which we are not yet aware.

If there is anywhere the perfect prototype of the legendary cave of Sawney Bean it can be very little better than the caverns of the Mendip Hills in Somerset, which consist of a number of vast underground caves reaching back into the hillside to a depth not yet fully known but at least as extensive as his. Through these caves flow streams which have gouged out underground lakes and chambers from the soft rock, forming over the centuries a living-place for man from the New Stone-Age to recent times, against a background of stalactites and stalagmites.

Since the skeleton of the "Cheddar Man" was found in 1903 these caves have fascinated archaeologists. Excavations in the Wookey Hole carried out continuously between 1946 and 1951 yielded seventeen human skulls, numerous bones and an amount of Celtic pottery, dating from the second century, from the bottom of the pools. Except for one, the skulls belonged to people between the ages of twenty-five and forty years. Two of these were female, but the overall picture suggests that they may have been offerings to the spirit of the water for, as in the case of the Tollund Man, none of the remains showed signs of violence.

The story of the Wookey Hole throws some light on the cave-theme of the legend of Sawney Bean for the early records reflect the awe-inspired attitudes of people towards caves in general. It was visited by William of Worcester in 1470 who described it:

> Below the parish at Wookey-hole, about half a mile from Wells, there is a certain narrow entrance where, at the beginning, is an image of man who goes by the name of the porter. . . . The hall is about as large as Westminster Hall, and there hangs from the vaulted roof wonderful pendula of stone. . . .
>
> There is a kitchen in a chamber near the entrance to the hall of an immense breadth, and roofed in stone, there is also a chamber called an ost, for the purpose of drying barley grain to make beer, etc., and the figure of a woman is there clad, and holding in her girdle a spinning distaff.

We must not permit ourselves to be misled by these bland references to Porter, Kitchen, Hall and Woman as though they were specific and factual, but remind ourselves how, even today, people torture their imaginations to attribute some particular shape to a natural feature of rock which it may or may not resemble. At the same time it must be noted that the description of "a woman" was the best that the imagination offered at that date.

A hundred years later it was described by the eminent Elizabethan scholar, William Camden.

> There is a cave or den far within the ground, wherein are to be seen certain pits and riverets. The place they call Ochie-Hole, whereof the inhabitants feign no fewer tales, nor devise less dotages, than the Italians did of their Sibyl's cave in the mountain Apenninus. The name no doubt grew of Ogo, a British word that betokeneth a den.[59]

Unfortunately Camden did not record the folk-tales of the local people, but his reference to the Greek myth of Aeneas and the Sibyl which they brought to his mind is of importance.

> She descended into the cave, and Aeneas followed. Before the threshold of hell they passed through a group of beings who are enumerated as Griefs and avenging Cares, pale Diseases and melancholy Age, Fear and Hunger that tempt to crime, Toil Poverty and Death—forms horrible to view. The Furies spread their couches there, and Discord, whose hair was of vipers tied up with a bloody fillet. Here also were monsters, Briareus with his hundred arms, Hydras hissing, and Chimaeras breathing fire.[60]

The scenes of the infernal regions of the underworld which followed were the prototype of Dante's *Inferno* and this gives us some idea of the tales which the local folk told to Camden. His use of the word "den" makes it clear that Holinshed's "den in Angus" was a cave.

Twenty years later James VI came to the throne of England and sometime after that the figure of a woman became known as the Witch of Wookey—as might have been expected. Celia Fiennes, the noted traveller, who visited and described the cave in 1697, makes it clear that the tradition was well established at that time.

> There is a lofty place they call the Hall and another the Parlour and another the Kitchen; the entrance of each one out of another is with greate stooping under rocks that hang down almost to touch the ground. . . . They fancy many Resemblances in the rocks, as in one place an organ, and in another 2 little babys, and in another part a head which they call the Porters head, and another shaped like a dog, they fancy one of the rocks resembled a woman with a great belly which the country people call the Witch which made this cavity under ground for her enchantments.[61]

She also mentioned echoes and noises in the Wookey-Hole, but a present-day archaeologist indicates that the final word has not yet been said on this subject

> The Great Cave of Wookey Hole is known for occasional queer noises, including some like the clashing of cymbals. It is now known that these noises are connected with the flood levels of the river, and their cause is one of the things it is hoped the diving operations will bring to light.[62]

Finally the story of the Witch of Wookey was written down in the form of a poem by Dr Harrington of Bath and published in *Euthemia or the Power of Harmony* in 1756. The story of the Witch had followed the same cycle as the legend of Sawney Bean, beginning with a pagan shrine and ending with a written version, which contained all the changes which had been incorporated in the folk-tale during the intervening seven hundred years. As Baring-Gould had written, "they may not resemble each other in much that is superficial, yet a critical eye can often perceive their radical identity."

Beginning with a simple, if superstitious, fear of spirits, death and enemies, the first and most important change was brought about by the Christian Church when, as part of its efforts to overthrow paganism, it branded these beliefs and practices as *evil*. This was an abstract and subtle idea superimposed on top of already existing fears of death, pain, torture, slavery and all the other aspects of the ancient world which promoted insecurity and dread in the individual. It was designed to turn people to God and the Church for protection and security. As the Church grew in strength pagan beliefs were considered anti-Christian or *heretical* and those people who held them were subjected to harsh persecutions which, eventually, in the hands of the Inquisition, became just as savage, primitive and bloody as the practices they were supposed to be eliminating.

These philosophies had originated in Europe, and had been maturing for about five hundred years before they found their way into Britain with the Norman conquest. Aildred and others who were well versed in these ideas could do no other than judge the Galwegians by their own standards—and their writings reflected their thoughts. The mental process which concluded (after following a tortuous path) that the proper punishment for Sawney Bean and Bloody Baker was burning and not hanging started from these philosophies. For hundreds of years afterwards it was considered that cannibalism and blood-practices were heresy, not murder, and that the punishment was burning.

The behaviour of the Galwegians did nothing to minimise any accusations of this sort which may have been made against them. They were savage and bloodthirsty by any standards. They were also independent which, on the one hand, cut them off from the rest of the country and retarded progress and the infiltration of new ideas and, on the other, made them a nation—a force to be reckoned with under a local king or leader. The latter aspect makes it clear that any possibility of James the First of Scotland being associated with Sawney Bean in a factual way was out of the question. Their inclination to pursue Border warfare with the English, even in the face of the declared policies of the King of Scotland, until the sixteen hundreds bolstered the poor reputation they already had, and made them many enemies in the northern counties of England.

It was during this period that the folk-tales—the household tales—were developing and being passed from generation to generation by word of mouth in every country in Europe. Arising from the revulsion now inspired by the heretical beliefs of the Celtic pagans, came the tales of the wicked ogres, giants, monsters, vampires, werewolves and ghosts. These were the personifications of evil, later to be equated to the devil, which brought about all the misfortunes of mankind by their evil powers; particularly death of the body and destruction of the soul. Associated with these early anti-Christ figures were other Celtic themes, heads (The Monster of Morar), wells (The Headless Horseman of Tynron Doon), human blood (Childe Rowland), and cannibalism (Mr Fox, Bloody Baker and Sawney Bean). The Underworld, later equated to Hell, was common to many of them and was in any case a theme of the greatest antiquity.

We may assume that the original version of the legend of Sawney Bean came into existence during this time. (Not quite in it's present form, of course, and he may even have been a quaintly shaped rock at the mouth of a cave under Bennane Head.) It was not fortunate enough, as was Mr Fox, to have a passing reference made to it by Shakespeare to authenticate it, but then Scotland had no equivalents to the Elizabethan poets and playwrights. The legend can only establish its authenticity and antiquity by internal evidence—the story radicals—or the work of the Brothers Grimm and their followers are meaningless.

The next major change came a little after the year 1500 when the European ideas about witchcraft were introduced into England and Scotland, and from this point a whole new series of folk-tales were introduced and (as in the case of the Witch at Wookey) many of the older ones were transformed. Witchcraft was now associated with cannibalism, both were heresy and merited death by burning. By far the most influential figure in the persecution of witches in Britain was James VI of Scotland and I of England. He provided the perfect opponent to Sawney Bean in the classical situation, where a folk-tale required a Jack the Giant Killer or Childe Rowland to epitomise the victory of good over evil.

James is so comparatively recent in history, and his activities are so well documented, that had these two legendary characters ever met in fact, there would have been ample records to tell of it. This leads us to the inevitable conclusion that, although Sawney Bean may have existed as a person (and we have read authentic accounts of cannibals in Scotland), by the year 1700 he had become as much a legendary figure as Robin Hood, William Tell or Hearn the Hunter. The folk-tale, which may have started out as simply as Jack the Giant Killer or the Morar Monster, had had the hero transformed into James the King and other embellishments had been added.

For all his influence as a witch-hunter, James was not a popular King in Scotland. An attempt was made on his life just before he departed for England in 1603 and the reformed church continued to persecute witches without his assistance. It seems unlikely that he was included in the legend to honour his name, but that portion of his reputation which was included was well known and understood in both Scotland and England.

On the whole it would appear that the final version of the legend was constructed as the print was set up for the press before the production of the original broadsheet. To gain some idea of the motivation involved we must look into the political and social state of the times—for on this would hang the acceptability and saleability of the broadsheet and the very purpose of producing it; the profit to be expected from it. The table at the end of this chapter attempts to show how historical events were piling up just after the year 1700, in a way which would make the legend topical reading.

There is much in favour of the theory that the broadsheet published by Jollie and Sons of Carlisle was the first to see print, because of the proximity of that town to Galloway. For hundreds of years the townsfolk had been involved in warfare with the "wild men of Galloway", their children had been captured and sold as slaves in Ireland and, as the only large Border town in

England, it had been used by the English kings as a jumping-off point for raids into Scotland and as often had been the butt of retaliations.

The folk-tales of Galloway would have been known in the Carlisle area, as well as the importance and influence of James VI and I. They would have heard of the deeds of the Laird of Lag, and others like him, from Covenanters fleeing south and the legends that grew from their hated memory.They would also have heard the following story which seems to be a Covenanter version of the story-root from which the legend of Sawney Bean sprang. It may have been true, McTaggart certainly believed it.

> CARLINES COVE on the west side of the Dee. When the Covenanters were being hunted, a poor man of the name of Dixon took up his abode in Carlines Cove, and lived the whole of the time that foul persecution lasted, on shell-fish he gathered on the sea-shore beside him, the which he found means to broil on a fire by night; thus he eluded the foes of his clan, the foes of God and man. The mouth of the cave is quite covered with brushwood; at the farther end or benmost bore of it, remains yet his seat—a square of sea-stone; on it I expected to find an inscription of some kind or other, but was deceived. The assmidden, and other remains of fire, to be met with, together with the general appearance of the cave, left no doubt on my mind that it had once been inhabited, and for a considerable time.[63]

He seemed to refer to the cave under Borness Point and we know from the excavations carried out fifty years later that it had been inhabited in the Iron-Age and probably later. The need in the minds of the Galwegians to identify Lag, and others, with the devil and the primeval evil ogre did not stop at creating special-to-purpose folk-tales, but also caused them to refurbish old ones in this way so that a set of Covenanter folk-tales was added to their culture.

It is highly indicative that the legend of Sawney Bean was published only in England during the first hundred years of its existence in print. Since it combined a sense of wonder, degradation of a traditional enemy and so many well-known aspects of folk-tale and history it must have been something of a best-seller. It would have been topical during the period after the Union of

England and Scotland (1707), when English gun-boats were still patrolling the Galloway coast to discourage Scottish trade with the colonies in North America, and later during that period of fear and apprehension when England was expecting an invasion from Scotland by which the House of Stewart was aspiring to regain the throne.

Another aspect of the events which contributed to the Union, and to the whole question of cannibalism in Scotland, was the famine caused by eight consecutive harvest failures during the 1690s, which reduced the population by about a third. There was a marked reduction in temperature throughout Europe between the fifteenth and eighteenth centuries which is sometimes called the "little Ice Age". The Frost Fair held on the frozen River Thames when it was covered with ice between December 1683 and February 1684 is a well-known event which indicated the severity of the winters.

The accompanying early autumn and late spring frosts, particularly in the north of Scotland, made the harvests fail again and again, and famine and death followed. People may well have turned to cannibalism or eating fresh corpses to keep themselves alive under such conditions, and the examples given for 1341 at Perth and 1460 at Angus could have been simple statements of fact. Many cases have been recorded, ranging from shipwrecked mariners to a plane-crash victim, which seem to suggest that men will still eat men when they have to choose between death and cannibalism.

Incidents of this sort may have occurred during the worst famine of all during the 1690s and although no records are available at the time this is written, they would have been known at that time and have contributed to the topicality of the broadsheet.

Accusations of cannibalism as a weapon of propaganda is very old indeed and was used during this period. It had been used during the Great Rebellion in England and was to be used again against the French during the Revolution. Against this background it may be believed that the legend of Sawney Bean was used as anti-Scottish propaganda. If so, it seemed to have some success, for the evidence shows that some people believed that the Scots ate children during the 1745 Rebellion.

At the same time, and quite independently of the Rcbellions, the growing wave of body-snatching was creating a morbid interest about the defiling of the dead in Scotland and elsewhere. The really skilful resurrectionists could remove a body from a grave with great speed and yet leave few traces so that magical means were sometimes suspected. Eventually the situation became so acute that the Scots themselves found it necessary to stand guard over their dead with shot-guns.

By the time of the trial of Nichol Brown, the Edinburgh cannibal and murderer, in 1754, the legend of Sawney Bean had become preserved between hard covers which were instrumental in keeping it from loss during the next two hundred years. Although John Nicholson did not print anything new in his *Historical and Traditional Tales*, he is to be commended for again drawing attention to the legend and returning it to its original setting of Galloway. From there Sawney has never looked back. The story inspired the romances of Prest and Crockett and the field of interest widened through reprinting and paraphrasing many times.

Few traditional tales evolve once they are held in the aspic of the printed word, but there are notable exceptions which have changed and broadened their form and passed from one media to another. Notably the vampire, the werewolf and the witch are the traditional figures which have provided material for numerous books, plays and films. But the cannibal—even a cannibal in deadly enmity with so noteworthy a King—seemed to be falling into a decline. Except for the paraphrase by C. E. Maine in 1967 little recent interest had been shown and the legend seemed to have nothing more to offer.

In 1969, however, Sawney Bean again captured the attention of a wide audience at the Edinburgh Festival when a play of that name was produced with such success that it was later transferred to the London stage.[64]

A Table of Historical Events Connected with the Development of the Legend of Sawney Bean

1563 Witchcraft Acts passed by Elizabeth I and Mary Queen of Scots.
1566 James VI of Scotland born.
1573 Trial and execution of Gamier, the French cannibal.
1591 The Fian Plot. James's life threatened by witchcraft.
1597 James publishes *Demonologie*.
1603 James becomes James I of England.
1604 James's Witchcraft Act passed.
1625 James dies. Charles I ascends the throne.
1645 The Battle of Philliphaugh.
1659 Nine witches burned at Dumfries.
1670 Law passed against Covenanters' gatherings.
1688 James II flees to the Continent.
1695 Famine reduces the population of Scotland by one third.
1698 Elspeth McEwen burned as a witch at Kirkcudbright.
1700 Sawney Bean broadsheet published. (approximate date)
1707 Union of England and Scotland.
1710 Body-snatching riots at Edinburgh.
1715 First Jacobite Rebellion.
1722 The last witch burned in Scotland.
1733 Bloody Lag dies.
1734 Sawney Bean appears in Capt. Johnson's book.
1736 All Witchcraft Acts repealed.

1743 The Presbytery objects to the repeal of the Acts.
1745 Second Jacobite Rebellion. Carlisle taken by Prince Charles.
1746 Mary Saunders burned in England for Petty Treason.
1750 Abraham Crighton, vampire.
1754 Trial and execution of Nichol Brown, Edinburgh cannibal.
1766 Ann Cruttenden burned in England for Petty Treason.
1789 French Revolution.
1790 Petty Treason Act repealed.

15

The Play

> But I—I belong to wicked mankind,
> To the communion of sinful flesh.
> My transgressions, my iniquities and sins,
> And the waywardness of my heart,
> Condemn me to communion with the worm
> And all that walk in darkness.
>
> *The Dead Sea Scrolls*

The desire of the reading public during the early 1800s for stories of the macabre stimulated the playwrights to turn their talents to producing Gothic chillers. Although founded in a tradition of no greater antiquity than that of the cannibal or werewolf, the vampire was considered to be the most suitable character for the stage and a number of plays based upon the vampire legend were produced at this time.

It is interesting to note that when *The Vampire* appeared on the Paris stage in June 1820, and the English version at the Lyceum, London in August 1820, it was set in Scotland and had the sub-title of *The Bride of the Isles*. J. R. Planché, who wrote the English libretto, later remarked that he had to adapt "a French melodrama, entitled *Le Vampire*, the scene of which was laid, with the usual recklessness of the French dramatists, in Scotland, where the superstition never existed. I vainly endeavoured to induce Mr Arnold to let me change it to some place in the East of Europe. He had set his heart on Scotch music and dress—the latter, by the way, were in stock—laughed at my scruples, assured me that the public would neither know nor care—and in those days they certainly did not."

His supposition that the vampire was unknown in Scotland was, as we have seen, ill-founded. The vampire in these, and later, versions was an English (rather than a Transylvanian) noble named Lord Ruthven. Presumably this prompted the name of the character Sir Ruthven Murgatroyd in Gilbert and Sullivan's *Ruddigore*.

The character of Count Dracula in Bram Stoker's book (1897) was a re-statement of the vampire legend in a setting of Eastern Europe, where writers had obviously been itching to set the vampire for about a hundred years. The success of this particular conception of the ancient legend cannot be denied, since it became a popular play in 1925 and is now a permanent feature of the movie-screen.

The interest aroused by the film presentation of gothic chillers in the early nineteen-thirties gave a new lease of life to old legends. The werewolf, the Golem and others appeared without the necessity of having first been a play. The Frankenstein monster, first conceived in 1818, was transposed directly from the pages of the novel with success.

The process of transferring a story from one media to another presents certain difficulties, but the large screen is better suited than the play to present out-door and rapidly moving scenes. The story of the vampire in its present form is the only one which adapts easily to the stage; the others had to wait for the film. The legend of Sawney Bean has not been transposed, but we may yet see the bloodhounds racing in full cry through the dripping caves and the final confrontation of Sawney and James in technicolor.

However, the legend of the vampire and others has been *progressive* while the legend of Sawney has tended to be *retrogressive*. It is a far cry from the rotting, pestilential *Vampire of Annan* to the elegant, wealthy *Count Dracula*—and yet the story radicals are obvious, regardless of the present sophistication of the story. Sawney, on the other hand, was presented at his most advanced in the broadsheet—as a notorious criminal of the seventeenth century. Subsequently versions by Prest and Crockett, depicted him as a primitive, and even Nicholson adjusted the text to set him in the fourteenth century.

In writing the play *Sawney Bean*, Robert Nye and Bill Watson completed this process, dropped the entire original action and set the scene on a beach before a cave. In doing this they were able to portray that which the historian cannot prove or demonstrate—the innermost thoughts and feelings of the characters. Much of the original atmosphere was retained; the cave and the beach dominated the scenery, and human limbs were supposedly cooked and eaten during the action of the play. It was the mental processes, however, which prompted their activities that the play sought to explore. In this way the themes of the age-old legend were shown in a new light, and Sawney Bean, the primitive man, emerged as a human and understandable figure.

In the second act Sawney, his wife, Lila, and his children, Solomon, Jot and Rain, sit outside the cave and feast upon his latest victim. He recalls in great detail various people he has killed and what passed between them before the killing. The relationship between the killer and the victim was important, as was the ritual dance which Sawney performed before the deed was done.

Referring to the food they are eating, Sawney says,

> You didn't know him. You had no talk with him. Look at you eating, you had no talk with that. You don't know what you're eating, but I know. I knew his flesh when its tongue still spoke. Its ears heard me speak. Its eyes saw me come. Its nose smelt its own fear. You just eat flesh, Solomon, all of you just eat flesh, but Sawney eats more than that.

Solomon, caught up in the mental anguish of adolescence, fears and respects Sawney; yet he decides to kill him to have Lila. In the following speech Solomon poses to himself all those questions which go hand in hand with ritual cannibalism and sympathetic magic, as well as the matter of incest which is inherent in the legend.

> He will last a long while. It will be a long meal, so I will put him down in salt, the biggest bits. First I shall have the heart and then the liver. What will they taste of? Will they taste different? Where will the questions be? He thinks they are in the blood. I think they are in the bone, juicy in the marrow, questions to suck and pry out with the tongue. And then what

> will it be like with me, with him in me, and me him walking, thumping on trees, bruising the clouds with my head, holding the wind in my fist, moving across the land, away from here, taking my Lila with me with his hunger and with mine.

In this way the play is threaded with the questionings of the primitive mind. It opens with a soliloquy from Sawney on the puzzle of existence. He speaks of a gigantic presence beneath the sea of which only he is aware, Lila recounts dreams of a childhood spent in a tropical paradise and Rain talks with a pool among the rocks.

The magic of a name as an integral part of the individuality (another aspect of sympathetic magic) is explored for Jot, the youngest, has no name until Sawney gives him one at the end of the first act.

> Sol. It's you. They're going to give you a name soon.
> Jot. Today?
> Sol. I think so. Rain thinks so.
> Jot. Why does he have to give us names?
> Sol. Don't you want to have a name then?
> Jot. I don't mind, but why does he do it?
> Sol. He likes naming things. He gives everything a name. But you're right. . . . I wonder why? He was the first of us, so perhaps it made him less alone to look at the sea and call it Sea, and to touch the rock and say Rock, and suck the air and say Air. Perhaps he spoke to them.
> Jot. Perhaps they spoke to him.

Sawney is finally killed when, in the darkess, he falls into a pit-trap dug by Solomon. With his dying breath he emphasises once again his primitiveness—his ability to smell a human being.

> Sawney Hey, hey, who's that? What's that Sawney? What's that smell? (Pause). I smell . . . Solomon!
> (Through the word "Solomon" SAWNEY falls down the pit, which is a long way. He land's on SOLOMON's bone-breaking stones, and is mortally damaged.)

The publishers of the play described it—

> Like all great myths, this beautiful and powerful fable, based

> on the true story of an eighteenth-century Galloway cannibal, touches on the reader's primal instincts and responds to his deepest needs for artistic expression. The characters are essentially timeless. . . . The play works on many levels and gives birth to many complex themes; poetically and imaginatively it examines the nature of innocence and knowledge, it poses questions about the meaning of religion and arising from this has a strong, driving ritualistic form and flow.

Apart from the assumption that Sawney existed in the eighteenth century, this is a fair statement of the content of the play. Despite the clothing of the characters they are truly timeless. Their thoughts, questions, doubts and suppositions are those which must have passed through the minds of those Stone-Age people who lived near the beach at Ballantrae. It was this very questioning of the relationship between themselves and the things about them which was the basis of primitive religion.

From this grew the reverence of caves, of streams and lakes; the magic of the attributes of the human body and their transference by the sympathetic magic of cannibalism and the secret magic of that intangible part of a person—his name.

But primitive man lived in fear and in the shadow of death, and from this grew the propitiation of spirits, ogres, ghosts, fairies and the souls of the dead which expressed itself in rituals—the human sacifice, the severed head, the goblet of blood.

Yet, for all the horror and revulsion we may feel, this was a kind of innocence. There was no evil in this—it was not wrong. Mankind was as a small child, at a stage where everything was new and unknown, to be touched, explored and tried. Knowledge came with experience and the road to civilisation was a steep and difficult path.

It was certainly not the fault of the Iron-Age people of Britain that the Christians from the south brought with them a better way of life. Their way of life was doomed in any case, it was only a matter of time. Yet it is human to cling to the familiar, and comforting to tell tales of the old heroes and ogres even though they would never be known again.

Thus the circle was completed when Sawney spread his arms and gazed across the footlights at the Traverse Theatre Club, Edinburgh.

Who?, he said, There is nothing, only me, and the sea. And the rock. And the black. And the grass. And the fire and stars and shells. And crabs and birds and seaweed. And the tree with all its leaves which are kind to me. And the rain, I like the rain.

Notes on Chapters

Chapter 2

1 The story of Maria Marten is true. She was murdered by William Corder on May 18th 1827. He was hanged the following year before a crowd, it is said, of 10,000 people who later filed past his naked corpse. His skeleton was kept in the court-house at Bury St Edmunds together with an account of the trial bound in his own skin. The rope which was used to hang him was sold for £1 per inch as mementos. A contemporary ballad published by F. Hodges of 26, Grafton Street, Soho, London, began the deluge of printed versions which, together with plays performed by second-rate companies, kept the incident to the forefront of public attention for over one hundred years. James Catnach's version, *Last Dying speech and Confession of the murderer of Maria Marten,* sold 1,166,000 copies. For further information on the changes in book publication at this time, see *The Long Revolution,* R. Williams, (Chatto & Windus), 1958

2 *Rogues Walk Here,* Wm. Roughead (Cassell), 1934

Chapter 3

3 *The Scottish Gallovidian Encyclopedia,* J. MacTaggart, London 1824

4 *Celtic Britain,* Sir J. Rhys (Soc. for Promoting Christian Knowledge), 1884

Chapter 4

5 *Failte romhat go h-Eirinn,* Vol. 17, No. 6

6 *Witchcraft and Second Sight in the Highlands and Islands of Scotland,* J. G. Campbell, 1900

7 *A Secret Commonwealth of Elves,* R. Kirk, 1691 (Ed. A. Lang, 1893)

Chapter 5

8 *The Scottish Gallovidian Encyclopedia*, J. MacTaggart, London 1824
9 *Statistical Account*, Wigtown 1841, Kircudbright 1845
10 *Witchcraft and Superstitious Record in the South-Western District of Scotland*, J. M. Wood (Maxwell), 1911
11 *A Description of the Sheriffdom of Wigtoun*, Sir A. Agnew of Lochnaw and D. Dunbar of Baldoon, 1850
12 *Old Statistical Account*, 1791–99
13 *Proceedings of the Society of Antiquaries of Scotland*, Vols. X, XI, and XII, 1908, 9 and 10
14 *Rambles in Galloway*, M. M'L. Harper (Frazer), 1896
15 *Proceedings of the Society of Antiquaries of Scotland*, Vol. LXXI, 1936–37
16 *The Stone Age in Scotland*, A. D. Lacaille (O.U.P.), 1954

Chapter 6

17 *The West Kennet Long Barrow*, excavations 1955–56, S. Piggott (H.M.S.O.), 1962
18 *Report on the Inhumation Burials from the West Kennet Barrow*, L. H. Wells, Appendix 1 to the above
19 *The Sunday Times*, Sept. 2nd. 1973
20 *Cannibalism and Human Sacrifice*, G. Hogg (Hale), 1958
21 *Illustrations of Northern Antiquities*, R. Jamieson, 1814
22 *Saints in Folklore*, C. Hole (Bell), 1966
23 *The Vampire: Its Kith and Kin*, M. Summers (Kegan, Paul, Trench & Trubner), 1928

Chapter 7

24 *The Saints of Hexham*, Aildred of Rievaulx (Raine's Hexham, Vol. I)
25 *Historia Anglorum*, Henry of Huntingdon
26 *De Gestis Stephani*, Richard of Hexham (Chronicles of Stephen, Vol. III)
27 *De Standardo*, Aildred of Rievaulx (Chronicles of Stephen Vol. III)
28 *Vita Thurstini Archiepiscopie*, (Raine's York)
29 *Description of Wales*, Giraldus Cambrensis, c. 1190
30 *Imagines Historiarum*, Ralph de Decito, Vol. I
31 *Historia Rerum Anglicarum*, Williams on Newburgh (Chronicles of Stephen, Vol. I)
32 *Chronica Majora*, Matthew Paris, Vol. III
33 *Gesta Henrich II*, Benedict of Peterborough, Vol. II

34 *The Scottish National Dictionary* groups the words BANE, BEEN, BEAN, BEIN and BAIN under one pronunciation; the word BEANE is not included. Nicholson converted Beane to Bean throughout his version and it will be noted that all Scottish writers used Bean. Apparently the use of Beane was introduced in England for no obvious purpose and the author has, except in quotation, used Bean in this book.

Chapter 8

35 *Caledonia*, G. Chalmers, 1807

36 *A History of the House of Douglas*, Sir H. Maxwell, Freemantle & Co. London 1902

37 *Scottish Chronicle*, R. Holinshed, 1577. Also mentioned in John of Fordun's *Chronicle of the Scottish Nation* which dates it 1339 and says they lived in a cave.

38 *Chronicles of Scotland*, Lindsay of Pitscottie (Ramsay), 1814. Holinshed also mentions this tale. "There was a certain thief that with his family lived apart from the compaine of men, remaining secretlie within a den in Angus, called Fenisden who used to kill young persons and feid on their flesh."

39 *Britain's Distemper*, Patrick Gordon of Ruthven (Spalding Club) 1844

Chapter 9

40 The attitude of the Church and State towards witchcraft is dealt with more fully in *Witchcraft in British History*, R. Holmes (Muller) 1974

41 *Unique Traditions of the West and South of Scotland*, J. G. Barbour, 1886

42 *The History of Galloway*, W. Mackenzie, 1841

43 *Teutonic Mythology*, J. Grimm (Dover Press), 1966

44 *The Hereditary Sheriffs of Galloway*, Sir A. Agnew, 1864

Chapter 10

45 *The Bard and the Belted Knight*, W. Johnstone (Elliot), 1867

46 *Notes on the Folk Lore of the Northern Counties of England and the Borders*, W. Henderson, 1866 (E.P.P.) 1973

47 *The History of Sanquhar*, Dr R. Simpson, 1853

Chapter 11

48 *Woodstock*, (Note III), Sir W. Scott (Ward Lock), 1833

49 *Bishop Burnet's History of His Own Time*, Vol. I, 1753

50 *The History of Civilisation in England*, H. T. Buckle, 1857 (O.U.P.) 1931

51 *Bishop Burnet's History of His Own Time*, Vol. II 1753
52 *The Scots Worthies*, John Howie, 1774
53 *Witchcraft and Superstitious Record in the South-western District of Scotland*, J. M. Wood (Maxwell), 1911
54 *The History of Scotland*, J. H. Burton, 1867
55 *Memoirs of the Rebellion in 1745–46*, J. de Johnstone (Longman), 1822

Chapter 13

56 *Highways and Byways in Galloway and Carrick*, Rev. C. H. Dick (MacMillan), 1916. The Rev. Dick incorrectly attributes this description to Sir H. Maxwell's *Evening Memoires*, (Maclehose 1932). Maxwell briefly mentions the story but gives no description.
57 *Rambles in Galloway*, M. M. Harper (Frazer), 1896
58 *Buried Treasure*, P. Johnstone (Phoenix House), 1957

Chapter 14

59 *Britannia*, Wm Camden, 1586
60 *The Age of Fable*, Thos. Bullfinch, 1855 (Dell Pub. Co.) 1972
61 *Through England on a Side-Saddle*, C. Fiennes, 1888
62 *The Mendips*, A. W. Coysh, E. J. Mason & V. Waite (Hale), 1971
63 *The Scottish Gallovidian Encyclopedia*, J. MacTaggart, 1824.
64 *Sawney Bean*, R. Nye & B. Watson (Calder & Boyars), 1970

Index

Book List

Dead and Buried? N. Adams (Impulse Books), 1972.

A Type and Motif-Index of the Folktales of England and North America, E. W. Baughman (Moulton), 1965. Indiana University Folk-lore Series No. 21.

The Glory of Scotland, J. J. Bell (Harrap), 1932.

English and Scottish Popular Ballads, Edited from the collection of F. J. Child by H. G. Sargent and G. L. Kitteredge (Harrap), 1904.

The Grey Man, S. R. Crockett (Fisher Unwin), 1896.

The World's Strangest Crimes, C. E. Maine (Odhams), 1967.

Historical and Traditional Tales connected with the South of Scotland, J. Nicholson, 1843.

Pagan Celtic Britain, Dr A. Ross (Routledge & Kegan Paul), 1967.

The Book of Galloway, J. A. Russell (Blacklock, Farries), 1962.

Witchcraft in the Middle Ages, J. B. Russell (Cornell U.P.), 1972.

Motif-Index of Folk Literature, S. Thompson (U.S.A.), 1955–8.

Acknowledgements

The author sincerely thanks those who have helped with this book, but who are too numerous to mention by name. Special thanks are due to Mr A. E. Truckell, M.B.E., M.A., F.S.A. (Scot.), F.M.A., Curator of the Dumfries Burgh Museum for information and advice, and to my wife for assistance with proof-reading, etc. Thanks are also due to Mr T. B. Brown of Glasgow who helped a complete stranger with an injured foot and then loaned him J. J. Bell's *Glory of Scotland*.